Developing New Brands

Developing New Brands

Stephen King

A HALSTED PRESS BOOK

John Wiley and Sons
New York

First published in Great Britain by Sir Isaac Pitman & Sons Ltd. 1973

Published in the U.S.A.
by Halsted Press
a division of John Wiley & Sons Inc.,
New York

ISBN: 0 470-47787-3

Library of Congress Catalog Card No: 72-14212

Text set in 10/11 pt. Monotype Times New Roman, printed by letterpress, and
bound in Great Britain at The Pitman Press, Bath
G3—(TML 13:51)

Preface

What makes companies succeed is not products, but brands. Arthur Guinness & Company prosper not because they brew stout, but because people want to drink Guinness. Lever Brothers are successful not because they make soaps and detergents, but because housewives like and buy Persil, Omo, Radiant, Surf, Lux and Lifebuoy. International Business Machines' dramatic growth has come not because businessmen want a computer, but because they want an IBM.

No one today would seriously doubt this. Yet all too often when companies are planning new ventures, they talk only about products; brands are hardly mentioned at all. All the discussions are about "new product development". This book is different: it is about developing *new brands*.

This is not just playing with words. The difference between products and brands is fundamental. A product is something that is made, in a factory; a brand is something that is bought, by a customer. A product can be copied by a competitor; a brand is unique. A product can be quickly outdated; a successful brand is timeless.

The conventional approach to new ventures classifies them on two dimensions—newness of technology and newness of market. New product development is seen as new technology in an existing market, and it is distinguished from diversification, which is seen as new technology in a new market. This is certainly one way of looking at it, but it misses the real point.

The real differences in approach for a company—in management, organization, planning, working methods and control—do not depend on whether the technology is new or the market is new. They depend on whether the company aims to get its growth from current brands or new brands.

A going brand has a firm base in its existing reputation and in people's direct experience of it. It can develop from this base with a series of modifications. Its penetration can be increased and its uses extended (new markets) or its product developed (new technology). Range extensions, product improvements, added services, new packs, new promotions and new advertising are all a normal part of marketing any going brand.

New brands simply do not have this firm base. Nothing about them is fixed. This means that inventing them is a radically different job from developing a going brand—whether they involve new markets and technology or familiar ones. The difference has implications both for management and for every department in a company. Increasingly, success will go to the company that understands the nature of the difference and acts accordingly.

That is why, if we want to succeed with new brands, we have to start right at the beginning and consider why it is that some new brands do well and some fail. What is wrong with much of today's practice is that it leaves out this stage: it is not based on any clearly worked out theory. However skilled the work and however valid the techniques, they will be useless if they are just flung together in a haphazard way. Only when they are part of a consistent philosophy and a continuous programme will they give good value.

So there are really three questions that need to be asked:

1. What makes new brands succeed?
2. How then should we organize to invent them?
3. What sort of programme of work do we need to plan them, develop them and evaluate them?

This book aims to provide some answers.

Contents

1   *What Makes New Brands Succeed?*

I t is by no means always clear why companies need new brands at all; or if they do, how many they need. Many companies are fairly ambivalent about it. On the one hand, the Chairman and others are fond of saying "New products are the life-blood of this company", and they wonder uneasily how long the profits from existing brands will keep up. On the other hand, their experience of new product development has often been unhappy; it upsets the routine of the company and the shareholders resent the money wasted on failures. So development work is allowed to drift on, but the funds voted to it are kept under strict control; nobody *acts* as if new products were the life-blood of the company. What usually emerges from this is a fairly large number of not terribly expensive new projects, most of which fail and the best of which are only moderate profit-earners. This middle course is the worst of all possible worlds.

There is little doubt that most new brands or products do fail. One Nielsen analysis[1] over fourteen years showed that 54 per cent of new products were withdrawn after test marketing; and presumably some of those that reached national distribution were later withdrawn too. Kraushar, Andrews and Eassie's 1971 study[2], based on Shaw's *Guide*, notes that 410 new food products (including range extensions, but excluding private label and four food categories) were introduced into the UK grocery trade in 1965; five years later 60 per cent of them had disappeared. A National Industrial Conference Board survey,[3] though

[1] A. C. NIELSEN COMPANY LIMITED, *How to strengthen your product plan*, 1966.
[2] KRAUSHAR, ANDREWS & EASSIE LIMITED, *New products in the grocery trade*, 1971.
[3] HOPKINS, D. S., and BAILEY, E. L., "New-product pressures", *The Conference Board Record*, June 1971.

apparently weighted in favour of major companies and more generally optimistic, still showed that in US consumer goods the failure rate for the median company was 40 per cent.

What is rather more significant is the extent to which *companies* fail in new markets. A 1965 J. Walter Thompson study[1] of 29 grocery and household product markets in the UK, also based on Shaw's *Guide*, showed that of the 294 company names entering these markets between 1954 and 1960, 49 per cent had already withdrawn by 1964. It is not as if the companies involved in these failures were inexperienced; most were marketing their established brands successfully enough. The same seems to be true of the US. In one list[2] of 75 new product failures in 1968, the companies responsible included Menley and James, Heinz, Campbell, DelMonte, American Home, Revlon, General Foods, Procter and Gamble, Colgate. (Of course, a lot of the successes also come from this sort of company.) Nor were most of the failures glorious bold attempts to introduce radical innovations, which failed because they were before their time. On the whole, the products were very similar to those already on the market.

Diagnoses[3] of the reasons tend to be interesting, but not very helpful. Certainly some of the causes of failure are basic incompetence in a specific skill; for instance, NICB surveys have stressed inadequate market investigations and shown that a particular problem in industrial machinery in the US was that of the new machine turning out to be less durable than the one it was designed to replace. But on the whole the analyses simply show that to be successful a new brand or product has to be "better" than existing ones.

If it is as hard as this for the most experienced marketing companies to develop new brands successfully, why develop them at all? Do all companies need them? If they do, how many do they need? How often do they need them?

WHY NEW BRANDS AT ALL?

The starting point for a new brand policy must be some consideration of what new brands are for and whether they really are necessary.

---

[1] DUNBAR, D. S., "New lamps for old", *The Grocer*, 3 April 1965.

[2] ANGELUS, T. L., "Why do most new products fail?" *Advertising Age*, 24 March 1969.

[3] e.g. A. C. NIELSEN COMPANY LIMITED, "The realities of new product marketing", *Nielsen Researcher*, January–February 1970; NAPIER, J. P., "What percentage of new products fail, and why?", *Advertiser's Weekly*, 5 November 1965; NATIONAL INDUSTRIAL CONFERENCE BOARD, "Why new products fail", *The Conference Board Record*, October 1964.

Until a company has worked this out, it will have no idea of the right scale of operations.

Three sorts of reason for trying to develop new brands have been put forward: the product life cycle, the demands of technological change and the need to grow.

The first is very largely bogus. It comes from a misreading of the product life-cycle theory. In simple terms, the theory says that any product's life is in four stages—introduction, growth, maturity and decline. In its original form, this is a respectable enough theory, and it has been shown[1] to be a fairly good description of what happens in a number of US markets. In a sense, it is bound to be valid, if taken to mean that every product introduced will reach a peak at some time and eventually disappear. The timing will differ, from sets of 1970 World Cup souvenirs, whose cycle might be complete in a year, to bread, which will take many centuries. The trouble has come when this innocent theory has been used operationally. People have said in effect: "Life cycles are getting shorter. Our brand's sales this year are lower than last year; it must be over the top, on the way to decline. We must introduce a great many new brands."

This way of thinking, which is very common, is really fallacious. The theory is descriptive and general; not predictive and rigid. *Above all it applies to products rather than brands.* It says that a product's sales will grow until the needs it meets are satisfied, after which it is likely to grow only as fast as the population with the needs grows; or until some other product emerges that will fill the needs better. Nearly all new products are new means of meeting existing needs. But there is absolutely no reason why a *brand* should not have its product changed or improved to meet its needs better. Only if the brand is rigidly unchanging will it be overtaken and suffer the decline suggested by life-cycle theory.

The astonishing thing is that in many companies whose growing profits over the years have depended almost entirely on one or two steadily growing brands there are marketing men who can ignore the evidence before them, in favour of their reading of the life-cycle theory. One result can be a self-fulfilling prophecy. The company's major brand has a bad year; so it is said to be in its late maturity stage; funds are withdrawn from it, both to make the most profit out of it while it lasts and to finance new brands; so the next year it does even worse; this confirms the original diagnosis and panic increases; new brands are hustled along faster and faster, and most fail; the company has talked itself into a decline.

[1] POLLI, R., and COOK, V. J., "Validity of the product life cycle", *Journal of Business*, October 1969.

Oxo cubes are a good example of the dangers of the life-cycle theory. Sales had reached a peak in 1948 and had tended to decline for the next ten years, despite the fact that until 1957 the price was held steady at one penny per cube—the same as in 1910. It would have been easy to

FIGURE 1. A challenge to life-cycle theory

argue that Oxo was at the beginning of the decline stage of its life cycle. It was old-fashioned and had had a good fifty-year run; its sales had notably reached a peak during both world wars, when meat was of poor quality and in short supply—hardly the situation in the new affluent UK. The company took the opposite point of view; it invested in Oxo in 1958–59. There was a new marketing management and a strengthened sales force; the cubes were completely repacked; a new unit size was introduced; rather more was spent on advertising and a new agency was appointed, with a new campaign and media plan. Five years later volume sales were up 35 per cent and the brand had become strong enough to stand two price increases. And six years after that, with the aid of a line extension, sales and profits reached new peaks. Against this, any major diversion of resources, through a naïve reading of life-cycle theory, could have ruined the company.

The second quoted reason for developing new brands is related to

4

life-cycle theory, but it is rather more reasonable. It is that techno-logical change is getting so fast that no single brand can keep up with it. Technological change means new products and eventually new products mean new brands. In other words, the number of new brands a company has to produce depends on its product innovation policy. There is a lot in this argument. In most industries, the rate of techno-logical change has accelerated and nowadays few companies could survive for long without some product innovation. Every time a new constructional material or new fibre or new chemical process or new method of food preservation or new control system is developed it will have repercussions over a huge range of companies.

At the same time, there is a long continuum of product innovation. At one end of the scale, there is the policy of a DuPont or an ICI which, backed by huge resources, sets out to create entirely new materials and product types—replacement for steel, replacements for natural fibres, new forms of energy source, new forms of medicine, synthetic protein and so on. At the other end of the scale, there is the sort of product innovation involved in adding a new green flavour to a range of jellies or changing from a bottle to a plastic squeeze-pack.

It is only a few of the largest companies that could afford to in-novate in the DuPont way. The research investment is enormous and most of the really striking technical advances—frozen foods, xero-graphy, transistors, penicillin, television—have taken a very long time to emerge as commercial propositions.[1] Any company following a product innovation policy towards this end of the scale must inevitably launch many new brands; the sheer number of technical develop-ments dictates it. Not only directly but also as a by-product of the major research projects. For instance, it was DuPont's research into refrigerants that produced, almost incidentally, the polytetrafluoro-ethylene used to coat non-stick frying pans.

However, most companies are much nearer the other end of the scale, and a policy of merely keeping up to date with technological change does not *necessarily* mean introducing new brands. The rate of change is often grossly exaggerated, and in practice most new products emerge gradually from modification of existing ideas and technology, from putting together familiar things in a slightly different way. All that most companies need in their existing markets is to make sure that their going brands join in the game of technological leapfrog.

In fact, the successful development of new brands does not neces-sarily require a higher degree of *technical* innovation than is needed for maintaining old brands. Many of the most successful new brands

[1] ADLER, L., "Time lag in new product development", *Journal of Marketing*, anuary 1966.

represent only minor advances over the products already on the market. Professor Levitt[1] has pointed out that the greatest flow of newness in products is not innovation at all, but imitation. He quotes IBM as imitators in computers; Holiday Inns in motels; RCA in television; Lytton in savings and loans. It is almost inevitable that most commercial ventures are based on product imitation and adaptation; there are a great many profitable brands and relatively few inventors and inventions.

The third reason for developing new brands is, for most companies, the only really valid one. Despite the costs and problems and risks, they need them in order to grow at the rate they have set themselves. This is true even where companies have grown by merger or acquisition. However successful their old brands are, there is usually a limit to the rate at which they can be expanded economically and there may even be a finite ceiling to the profits they can generate. Although very often in the short run investment in existing brands brings in a better return than the same amount spent on new brands[2], the new brands are needed to give a broader base for profits in the long run.

HOW MANY NEW BRANDS?

This analysis has important implications for development policies. If the primary reason for new brands is to build *long-term* sales and profits, then most companies need occasionally to develop a significant new brand. But only occasionally. Most of the time their technical innovation skills will be better used in keeping existing brands up to date, improving or replacing the physical products that are part of those brands.

Most companies find that a huge proportion of their profits comes from one or two well-established brands. If they want to build their profits for the future, then logically they should be trying to develop something similar—another important brand which, maybe from a modest start, gradually emerges as a sustained profit-earner. And yet so often they appear to be looking for something completely different in their new brands—a large number of instant successes. They seem to ignore what it is that has made them successful so far.

The real object of a development programme is to develop a *successful new business*, not to put a lot of new brands on the market. That does not require, and it is not helped by, a state of constant panic.

[1] LEVITT, T., *The marketing mode*, p. 54 (New York, McGraw-Hill Book Company, 1969).
[2] VAN CAMP, R. W., "Essential elements for new product success", p. 7, in *New product development* (American Marketing Association, 1968).

It is not helped by keeping hundreds of projects going, in the hope that by the law of averages one of them will hit the jackpot.

Looking on the object of the exercise as building a new business can transform the company's whole approach. The mystiques of new product development become less frightening. It becomes a more straightforward matter of sensible analysis, proper planning and the application of the right resources. Concentration on developing only a very small number of new brands can dramatically cut down the failure rate. The whole of this book is really about building a new business, by inventing one good brand.

THE PRODUCT AND THE BRAND

Running through all these arguments is the critical distinction between the product and the brand.

This is hardly a new idea; the importance of branding was generally realized nearly a century ago. Gardner and Levy's classic paper "The product and the brand" appeared in 1955.[1] And, although there are fuzzy areas, the distinction is a fairly obvious one. Yet the whole emphasis, both in the literature and in practice, has been on developing *new physical products*. Manufacturers of industrial goods especially seem to feel that brands are relevant only to consumer goods and are maybe a reflection of the illogical world of women; in the honest, tough world of heavy industry what are bought and sold are products. This is of course entirely false. The number of pure commodity markets is tiny. Every other market is one in which manufacturers are competing with brands—unique, named articles—whether they are brands of cosmetics or brands of refrigerator or brands of packaged travel or brands of machine tool.

Brands and branding are going to become more and more important[2]; failure to distinguish between product and brand in development work is going to get increasingly expensive. Of course, brands always have been important, and in the UK they were the means for manufacturers of breaking away from domination by the wholesalers at the end of the nineteenth century. But the long period of manufacturer domination, roughly up to the middle 1960s in the UK, is showing signs of ending and it will only be by success at branding that manufacturers will continue to show growth in profits. Conditions in the 1970s and beyond are going to be much tougher. There is far less

[1] GARDNER, B. B., and LEVY, S. J., "The product and the brand", *Harvard Business Review*, March–April 1955.
[2] KING, S. H. M., *What is a brand?* (J. Walter Thompson Company Limited, 1970).

scope today for concentration in numbers of manufacturers—most markets are already dominated by less than five—or for increased profits through economies of scale. The seller's markets of the immediate post-war era have come to an end. Retailers have gained enormously in power, especially where—as in the UK—resale price maintenance is banned. International competition is growing. And buyers show every sign of becoming much more discerning.

These trends have been particularly clear in the grocery trade. Nielsen have shown[1] that on the whole, where brands have been strongly established (that is, mainly the brand leaders), they have tended to gain market share and can command a substantial price premium. Equally, it is clear that cheap private-label brands have grown rapidly over the past five years. What this has clearly meant is a very severe squeeze on both the sales and the price level, hence profitability, of the weaker manufacturers' brands.

The same thing is happening in consumer durables and in industrial markets. Buying power is being concentrated, perhaps a little more slowly, over the whole retail trade. In the most technically advanced industries, Government contracts are becoming more important and Government buying methods tougher. And of course the buyers of most industrial goods are themselves manufacturers; as they grow and merge they will develop greater buying power.

Manufacturers in fact are likely to face increasing pressures—through increasing competition, pressure from their buyers and the rapid copying of their physical products (as happens with private-label brands). In this situation their profits will depend critically on the difference between the product and the brand. For their *products* they will get the commodity price, giving them a fairly low margin, and then only if they are efficient. For their *brands* they will get the commodity price plus whatever the brand is worth beyond the product. That is, the level of profits will depend on the values added[2] by the brand.

Hard as it may be for established brands, it is likely to be even harder for the new brand. Unless it can have added values built into it from the start, it is unlikely to be successful in building a long-term business. Just what these added values are and how to get them is central to what makes a new brand successful.

[1] A. C. NIELSEN COMPANY LIMITED, "Manufacturers' advertised brands", *Nielsen Reseacher*, July–August 1970; A. C. NIELSEN COMPANY LIMITED, "Cost of leadership—today and tomorrow", Nielsen Researcher, January–February 1963.

[2] MAYER, M., *Madison Avenue, U.S.A.*, p. 309 (New York, Harper & Row, 1958; p. 320, London, Penguin Books, 1961); YOUNG, J. W., *How to become an advertising man*, p. 69 (Chicago, Advertising Publications Inc., 1963).

WHAT ADDED VALUES?

In fact, what makes a new brand successful is becoming like an old one. We should stop worrying so much about how to launch new brands (the launching is really not very difficult), and concentrate on how to invent an established brand. Our models should be brands like Persil, Kellogg's Corn Flakes, Weetabix, Guinness, Bird's Eye, Oxo, Kit-E-Kat, Heinz soups and baked beans in the UK, Campbells soups in the US, Lifebuoy, Nescafé, Maxwell House, Kodak, Polo mints, Parker pens, the Cortina, Xerox, IBM. They may have had their ups and downs, but all these have established themselves strongly enough to bring in good profits over many years. They were all new brands once.

What do they have that lesser brands do not? Clearly they have had a high standard of production efficiency, control and day-to-day marketing. But that is true of many brands which, though fairly successful, are nowadays increasingly having their profit margins reduced. What is it that the really successful brands have that is extra? What are their added values?

We can get some insights by examining one particular post-war brand, which was first marketed on a large scale in the middle 1950s,

FIGURE 2. Andrex: a triumph for added values

9

became brand leader in 1961, and has remained leader ever since. The brand is Andrex, the first nationally branded soft toilet paper in the UK. Papermaking itself is complex and highly capital intensive; but the finishing production process—paper converting—is not terribly difficult and can be started up on a very small scale. And this is a market in which, for obvious reasons, the marketing man is limited in all sorts of ways.

It might easily have become a near-commodity market, *had the major manufacturer let it*. There are many less obvious markets which have become virtually commodity markets through the main manufacturers failing to realize the values of branding—the UK concentrated soft drink market, for instance.

Andrex was on the market in the 1940s, but its real growth started after Bowater–Scott was formed in 1956 and took over the originating company, St. Andrew's Mills. Its main direct competitor was Kimberly Clark's Delsey.

The introduction of soft toilet paper had greatly increased the total market (previously made up of the traditional "hard" paper), and by 1961 the prospects looked good enough to tempt in other manufacturers, both large and small. Private label and price-cutting started earlier here than in most markets; and as both Andrex and Delsey had started off with chemists' retail margins (grocery shops only started selling toilet paper in a big way in the UK in the early 1960s), there was plenty of scope for price-cutting. In fact, the retail price of toilet paper declined during the second half of the 1960s.

By 1963, the two new brands had made good progress. Andrex had a 22 per cent share of market volume, and that was enough to make it clear brand leader. Delsey was not far behind, with 16 per cent. But they were coming under increasing pressure from the retail trade, particularly the rapidly growing multiples. And from that time on the two manufacturers diverged in their response.

One effect of the retailer pressure was that most manufacturers switched their marketing funds from media advertising into trade discounts and promotions. That is, increasingly they were cutting their prices, selectively, to certain retailers; they were accepting lower margins. The net sales value per case of their brands decreased, and they were making up for it by cutting their marketing budgets and their links with the consumer. But there was a great difference between Andrex and Delsey here. By the end of 1965, Delsey had virtually stopped advertising and was concentrating almost entirely on discounting. Andrex kept a balance between the two, even though its advertising expenditure remained at a relatively low level.

The results of these policies were quite dramatic. The cheaper brands of soft paper gained share rapidly. Andrex continued to grow steadily. Delsey slipped back to its share of 1960.

By 1969 Andrex had reached a dominating 31 per cent share of market value and was strong enough to hold a retail selling price well above the market average. Throughout the period it contributed a high proportion of Bowater–Scott's profits. It did this in the face of considerable pressure from retailers, at the time when retail price maintenance was abandoned, when the retail selling price of toilet paper was declining and when multiples were growing very rapidly. The reason was that retailers needed Andrex, because it had been made in this relatively short period into a brand that *consumers valued highly*.

Continuous attitude research showed just how consumers' ideas of the relative values of Andrex and Delsey changed. Up to 1966 the two brands were advancing at much the same rate; indeed Delsey's

Changes in attitude to Andrex and Delsey

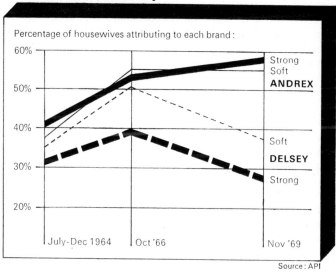

FIGURE 3. Delsey's reputation for softness and strength declined after stopping advertising in 1965

reputation kept up much longer than its market share. But after that time Andrex continued to advance, while Delsey's reputation for qualities like softness and strength declined. In fact, there was no evidence that objectively the standards of the two physical products

11

diverged in any significant way. Nor is it likely that people suddenly felt that Delsey was not as soft or as strong as it used to be, or that Andrex had got stronger or softer. What seems to have happened is that people simply valued Delsey, as a brand, a little less highly than they used to, Andrex a little more highly.

If Andrex developed more added values—values beyond the physical, functional ones of the product—where did these values come from? It seems clear that there were many sources, all blended into an overall impression of greater value. First, Andrex's early leadership in soft toilet paper and in innovations such as a colour range. The pioneer can clearly get a considerable advantage, if marketed properly. For instance, one Nielsen analysis[1] of 27 grocery fields showed that, after a minimum of three years on the market for any brand, the pioneer brand was selling on average more than twice as much as the first "me too" brand and nearly four times as much as the second "me too" brand. But that was not the whole answer, because the pioneering advantage wears off in time. Andrex did sell roughly twice as much as Delsey in 1958, but only 40 per cent more in 1963 when their promotional policies diverged. By 1969 it was about three times as much. Secondly, consistently high quality in product and packaging material. Thus good value for money. Again, while this could explain Andrex's success, it could hardly explain the pattern of brand shares after 1963. Delsey was strong there too, and indeed pioneered the polythene pack. Thirdly, Andrex's direct relationship with the final consumer, the housewife. It is not only the fact that Andrex continued to advertise, while Delsey did not. It is the way in which Bowater–Scott used advertising and packaging and merchandising; the way in which Andrex talked to the consumer. Or, to broaden it a little, the consistent way in which Andrex and its values were presented to the public *as a brand*. This was clearly a crucial element in the success.

We can get an idea of the values and strengths of Andrex as a brand by looking at its advertising over the years. There have been many different campaigns, no doubt of differing efficiency, created by different people, adapted by different people, judged and accepted by different people. Different media have been used. Some have concentrated on the softness of the product; some on the strength; some on both; some on neither. Superficially they vary a lot, and yet through them there is a great consistency. *They were dominated by the personality of Andrex itself.* What runs through them is not any unique product claim or unique feature or functional description.

[1] A. C. NIELSEN COMPANY LIMITED, "Seven keys to a strong consumer franchise", *Nielsen Researcher*, May–June 1962; "Some new guidelines for developing the product line", *Nielsen Researcher*, January–February 1966; *How to strengthen your product plan*, 1966.

It is an attitude of mind and a tone of voice and a set of values that belong to Andrex. Andrex emerges as having a clear personality. She is reliable, dainty, clean-living, domesticated, family-centred; she radiates niceness and confidence in her ability to manage. It is this that makes Andrex, as it were, a nice person to have about the house.

It seems clear, in fact, that Andrex has succeeded as a new brand and a profit-earner because it has added values beyond the physical and functional ones. These added values have contributed to a clear and likeable personality for the brand.

The same is true of many of the more successful new brands in the UK since the war; an element of pioneering, good quality product (but not necessarily outstanding) and added values through communication. Bird's Eye pioneered frozen foods, with product quality higher than people were used to in processed food and with a personality combining efficiency, hygiene, confidence and completeness; the three elements together have given it a massive share of market for fifteen years. Lucozade, a fairly simple glucose mixture with the sort of personality that some people like in a sickroom. Ribena, a blackcurrent cordial, with the personality of a young mother hopeful for the success of her children. Babycham, a fairly conventional perry, given a totally new personality by its advertising and packaging. After Eight mints, the combination of a new sort of peppermint cream, a high quality product and a highly distinctive personality, expressed in every contact with its public. It is easy enough to add to this list: Camay, Vesta, Ariel, Embassy, Fairy toilet soap, G-Plan, the Mini, Moulton bicycles, Instamatic cameras, Angel Delight. The balance between the elements of product innovation, product quality and brand personality varies; but in every case the successful result has been a blend of the three.

It is easy to assume that this only applies to consumer goods, maybe even only to fast-moving grocery goods. Certainly there are differences of degree, but the principle applies to industrial goods too. An industrial brand will not work as well if it relies solely on product innovation or product quality; to be successful it must have added values and a brand personality. Even patents are not normally a great protection against rapid copying; most patents are highly specific and it is difficult to close all loopholes which might allow in a competitor with a copy plus minor adaptation. It is an illusion that the makers of industrial goods do not need added values. Any mechanical or electronic product needs to be backed with the values of reliability and efficient after-sales service. And as industrial products become more complex, the added values will become more important; just as for the housewife today after-sales service may become the most important feature of the washing machine. IBM has dominated the computer business, not necessarily because its products are more innovative or functionally better than those of other computer manufacturers; but because an IBM computer represents advice and aid on uses for computers, programming services, advice on information systems, training programmes and a whole mass of instructional material. More than that, IBM has a personality which reflects zeal and self-regard so powerfully that it is hard to believe that it would allow itself to be seen to be inefficient. The IBM personality has deeply affected its employees; and as a result it is very rarely seen as inefficient. It has pursued added values harder than the others, and has reaped the reward.

The fact is that practically all goods are bought on the basis of repeat purchase or re-ordering. Obviously most consumer goods are, but it is true of industrial goods too. Thus the values of the new brand will nearly always depend to some extent on previous experience. The reputation of the manufacturer of a new industrial product is not just a factor affecting it; it is part of the new product—an added value. Levitt talks of the "augmented-product concept" and sums it up neatly[1]:

> Whether the product is cold-rolled steel or hot cross buns, whether accountancy or delicacies, competitive effectiveness increasingly demands that the successful seller offer his prospect and his customer more than the generic product itself. He must surround his generic product with a cluster of value satisfactions that differentiates his total offering from his competitors'. He must provide a total proposition, the content of which exceeds what comes out at the end of the assembly line.

Brand personality is perhaps a less abstract term than "cluster of value satisfactions", but it expresses the same notion of a range of attributes fused together. The Andrex case-history suggests that people do choose their brands in the same way that they choose their friends. There are degrees of friendship, and people very rarely stick exclusively to just one friend; in the same way there are degrees of brand loyalty, very rarely loyalty to one brand alone. Friendships come and go, according sometimes to what the friends say and do. Not everyone will like the same person, though some are more popular than others. People do not usually choose their friends solely because of specific skills or physical attributes, although such things can be very important. They usually choose them because, in addition to the skills and physical characteristics (or maybe in spite of them), they simply like them as people. It is the total person that is chosen as a friend, not a compendium of virtues and vices. The choice and use of brands is just the same.

[1] LEVITT, T., *The marketing mode*, p. 2 (New York, McGraw–Hill Book Company, 1969).

To some people the whole concept of brand personality might seem a rather fanciful way of describing why one brand is valued more than another. But there is overwhelming evidence[1] that non-functional values sway people's choices—evidence from blind $v.$ named product tests, pack testing, the placebo effect, the Hawthorne experiments[2], as well as most experimental psychology. Just as it is a fact that in industry the contract does not by any means always go to the company that meets the strict specification at the lowest cost.

There is also some direct evidence on brand personalities. Pilot research by J. Walter Thompson has made it quite clear that brands do have personalities and that people can talk fluently about them. Indeed talking about brands as people rather than things usually brings out a much richer vocabulary. These brand personalities tend to be consistent, though what is one person's praise is another's condemnation. For instance, Persil was seen by some as happy and contented; by others as dull and lacking in ambition—two facets of the same personality.

As people become richer, added values and brand personalities are likely to become more important to them. They will get more and more of their rewards in life from the non-functional. One man will get them from listening to a string quartet; another from polishing the "unnecessary" trim on his new car. Clothes are an example of the trend. They are no longer mainly for protection; they are more a demonstration of one's personality and values or of how one wants to be perceived. It was always true of high fashion; now it is true of mass-market clothes. The added values here have become more important than the functional, and this will become increasingly true of other product types. People will require style as well as performance. They will increasingly value brands for *who they are* as much as for *what they do*.

This theory of added values is critically important for new brands. It suggests that no new brand can hope to succeed if it does not have values beyond the functional. But it goes rather further than that. The added values are not simply something lumped on to the brand once the functional features have been settled. They are an integral part of its personality, its essence, its *raison d'être. The new brand must be conceived as this totality of functional and non-functional values from the very beginning.*

The idea of added values certainly comes mainly from looking at old-established brands. But applying it to the development of new

[1] KING, S. H. M., *What is a brand?* (J. Walter Thompson Company Limited, 1970).

[2] *see* BROWN, J. A. C., *The social psychology of industry*, p. 69 ff (London, Penguin 1954).

15

brands is more than just a theoretical leap in the dark. In fact, it illuminates all that we know about how new brands actually do behave. The importance of these added values emerges clearly from analysis of hard factual data.

HOW DO NEW BRANDS BEHAVE?

Today there is enough general information, from retail audits and consumer panels, to show fairly clearly how new grocery products behave. The evidence is that, despite great diversity of product type, there are some typical patterns of sales of new brands which show what is important to success and what is less important.

Retail Audit Data

An analysis by E. J. Davis[1] of 44 test market operations for consumer goods in the Southern, Tyne-Tees and South Wales television areas, using BMRB Retail Audit data, showed how distribution gradually builds up for new brands. There was a fairly smooth curve in cumulative distribution, with the "shoulders" of the curve reached on average in about three months. In these particular 44 cases the mean distribution at this shoulder was 35 per cent of grocers' shops handling. A Nielsen analysis of 29 new brands[2] showed the same pattern, with a mean sterling distribution of about 38 per cent in grocers at the shoulder, after six months. (The small discrepancy between the Nielsen and the BMRB figures can be largely accounted for by interpretation of what is the shoulder.) After this point, distribution increased at a much slower rate, reaching an average of 43 per cent in the Nielsen sample after twelve months. There were quite wide differences between brands judged by Nielsen to be successes and those judged to be failures; at the shoulder, the distribution of the successes was about 20 percentage points higher than that of the failures, and after that the gap got wider. In other words, the success or failure of the brand was apparent after only a few months (Fig. 4, opposite).

There are two important implications from these findings. The first is that reasonably good distribution is correlated with success. But this is not to say that it is the *cause* of success; it seems rather more likely that it is the *result* of success. In the Nielsen analysis the gap between

---

[1] DAVIS, E. J., *The sales curves of new products* (Market Research Society Conference, 1964, and J. Walter Thompson Company Limited, 1965).

[2] A. C. NIELSEN COMPANY LIMITED, "New product distribution levels", *Nielsen Researcher*, January–February 1969; "The realities of new product marketing", *Nielsen Researcher*, January–February 1970.

16

successes and failures was less in multiples and co-ops than in independents—indeed some failures achieved better initial distribution than some successes. This and the fact that the gap only really opened up after about four months both suggest that distribution varies mainly according to how well or badly the brand performs. The second implication is that any new brand will have to make its mark in the first month or two when it is not very widely distributed.

These distribution figures are a background to the findings of the Davis study on consumer purchases of new brands. There was a typical pattern here too. Consumer purchases rose fairly quickly to a peak, then declined to a relatively stable volume, from which growth (where it came at all) tended to be gradual. In half the 44 cases the peak level of consumer purchases was reached in the third four-weekly audit period, and it was usually (but not always) in the same period as the brand reached the shoulder of its distribution curve. Virtually all the new brands had reached their peak of consumer sales by the fourth audit period—that is, around fourteen weeks after they were launched.

The decline from the peak to the stable level took rather longer, but three-quarters of the brands had stabilized six months after introduction and the rest within eight months. A key finding from the analysis

£ Distribution of new products
Shops weighted for turnover importance

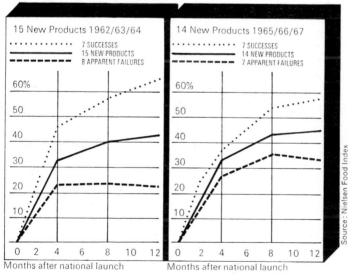

FIGURE 4. Nielsen show a link between distribution levels and success or failure for new brands

Consumer purchases of new brands

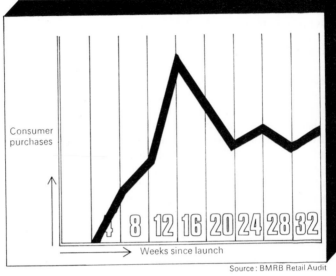

FIGURE 5. **Typical pattern of consumer purchases for new brands (Davis)**

was that the "drop" factor—the percentage decline from the peak to the stable level—appeared to be the same for a brand in all its test marketing areas, even though the levels of peak consumer sales differed widely. In other words, the amount of drop is related to the brand itself rather than to external factors like regional differences, competitors or differing sales skills.

The only really credible interpretation of these characteristic patterns shown by retail audit data is that a lot of initial buyers of the new brand come in during the first three months or so, as distribution climbs to its shoulder. As JWT's *New Housewife* survey[1] showed, the most frequent source of learning about new brands is through shop display or retailers' recommendations. But some of these new buyers continue to buy very infrequently, and some do not buy again at all. During the next three months or so the drop in consumer sales, caused basically by the lack of repeat-buying by disappointed triers, is offset to some extent by some more people becoming buyers for the first time; this is one reason why the decline from peak to stable is more gradual than the climb from nothing to peak. But by six months or so after the launch, new first-time buyers have ceased to be a *major* factor.

[1] TARRANT, M., *The new housewife*, p. 94 (London, J. Walter Thompson Company Limited, 1967).

18

The brand has settled down and consumer sales depend on the established repeat-buying rate. Growth from now on, in distribution, consumer sales, new buyers and the repeat-buying rate will be gradual. That is, unless the manufacturer takes action so dramatic as to alter all the patterns.

Consumer Panel Data

There has been a great deal of analysis of household buying data for new brands, from the MRCA consumer panel in the US and the Attwood panel in the UK.[1] On the whole, the findings support this interpretation of retail audit data. There is a characteristic curve of cumulative penetration for a new brand; that is, of households ever buying it. This penetration curve reaches its shoulder relatively quickly—in the case of 24 new grocery brands studied by Attwood it was within six months of introduction. One US analysis suggests that the shoulder is related to the number of new buyers attracted during the fourth average buying cycle; that is, at the point of time from launching that is three to four times the average interval between purchases of the product type. (The interval will, of course, vary from product to product—it might be two weeks for tea and two months for canned peaches.) After that growth is much slower, but the evidence is that there will be a fairly regular small gain for years, from new triers and new households. Thus after a brand has been on the market for five years or so it is quite common for the number of households buying it during, say, three months to be a relatively small proportion of those who have ever bought it. But the vast majority of buyers within the first year or two will have bought it during the three or four months after its introduction (Fig. 6, page 20).

The curve of the repeat-purchasing rate is the converse of this. Parfitt and Collins' analyses of Attwood data for 24 new brands showed that it tends to start off high and reaches a lower stable level after about three or four months. These two curves, of penetration and repeat-purchasing, had reached sufficiently stable levels after six months to allow extremely accurate forecasts of brand share twelve to eighteen months later.

The implication of this is that, in the new brand's first few months,

[1] AHL, D. H., "New product forecasting using consumer panels", *Journal of Marketing Research*, May 1970; FOURT, L. A., and WOODLOCK, J. W., "Early prediction of market success for new grocery products", *Journal of Marketing*, October 1960; PARFITT, J. H., and COLLINS, B. J. K., "The use of consumer panels for brand-share prediction", *Journal of Marketing Research*, May 1968; WOODLOCK, J. W., "A model for early prediction of a new product's future", *Commentary* (now *Journal of the Market Research Society*), summer 1964.

19

Cumulative penetration of brand Y

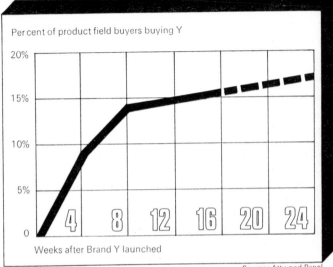

Per cent of product field buyers buying Y

20%

15%

10%

5%

0

Weeks after Brand Y launched

Source: Attwood Panel

Repeat·purchasing of brand Y

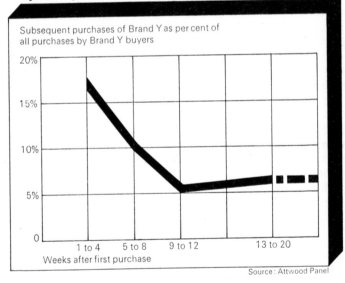

Subsequent purchases of Brand Y as per cent of all purchases by Brand Y buyers

20%

15%

10%

5%

0

1 to 4   5 to 8   9 to 12   13 to 20

Weeks after first purchase

Source: Attwood Panel

FIGURE 6. Typical pattern of growth in number of households trying a new brand; and typical decline in repeat-purchasing rate (Parfitt and Collins: *Journal of Marketing Research*)

there is a rapid influx of the most interested buyers, who continue to buy fairly frequently. The less interested are also coming in, but more gradually; they buy less frequently, and thus dilute the total repeat-buying rate. The uninterested—those who do not become buyers in the first six months or so—may not try the new brand for several years, if ever. This interpretation is directly confirmed by case-history studies on the Attwood panel, which showed that on average the sooner the buyer enters the market for a particular brand, the higher will be that buyer's repeat-purchasing rate. The early buyers have a disproportionate influence on the brand's ultimate market share. Thus, although dramatic marketing activities, such as massive promotions or price-cutting, can sometimes improve the cumulative penetration of the new brand, the extra buyers gained tend to have a relatively low repeat-purchasing rate. Parfitt and Collins' general impression was that "it is comparatively easy, within limits, to influence cumulative penetration, but it is extremely difficult to create or influence repeat-purchasing for any length of time". Their conclusions about the reasons for failure of a new brand made much the same point: "Failure generally takes the form of exceptionally low repeat-purchasing rates; that is, the brand makes a reasonable penetration into the market but very few people continue to buy it."

In time, it should be possible to compare the behaviour of new brands with the "norms" of consumer buying established by Ehrenberg[1]. The two case histories published so far by him suggest that it can take a long time for a new brand to settle into the buying pattern of its market. A tentative conclusion from the data is that the difference in pattern for new brands is due to irregularity of buying as much as to infrequency.

Survey Data

Continuous attitude information shows the same sort of picture. Data from the Advertising Planning Index on the introduction of Golden Oxo showed that penetration of households reached a first shoulder at 17 per cent after about six months. It was then sharply increased to 37 per cent by sampling and coupon distribution. However, the number of housewives saying they had bought more than once followed the characteristic penetration curve, only reaching 17 per cent some eighteen months after introduction. In other words,

---

[1] EHRENBERG, A. S. C., "Towards an integrated theory of consumer behaviour", *Journal of the Market Research Society*, October 1969; "Predicting the behaviour of new brands", Paper read at American Marketing Association conference, September 1970; EHRENBERG, A. S. C., and GOODHARDT, G. J., "Repeat-buying of a new brand", *British Journal of Marketing*, autumn 1968.

the majority of those brought in by sampling or coupon were once-only buyers.

The Total Appeal

One clear conclusion emerges from all these analyses: the new brand tends to set its own pattern. The quickly reached stable level of consumer sales depends mainly on how many people are interested enough to try it in the early months and how the first triers react to it. The regularity of the drop factor, the crucial importance of the repeat-purchasing rate and the tendency of the important buyers to come in first all point to one thing. What makes for success is the *nature of the brand.* No amount of marketing skills or forced distribution or massive promotions can do much for a brand whose total appeal is not quite right.

At first sight, it may not seem very startling to conclude that success or failure depends on how satisfied the consumer is with the brand in use. But in fact it shows us where to concentrate. The actual business of launching and distributing the brand can, if it is done badly enough, make the brand fail; but, however well it is done, it cannot by itself make the brand succeed. And bearing in mind that it is very rare indeed for a brand to be launched when its physical product is noticeably *worse* than existing competitors', it seems that product parity or minor product improvement is not enough to ensure success. What really seems to matter in the market-place is the *total range of satisfactions* that the new brand offers its early and most interested triers.

ANATOMY OF THE SUCCESSFUL NEW BRAND

Working out why the old-established brand leaders continue to bring in the profits and analysing the ways in which successful new brands actually start to build up their sales make it clear that there are certain essential ingredients for success. They seem straightforward enough, but their implications can have a dramatic effect on the way in which companies set their new brand objectives, the sort of organizations they need, their whole approach to development problems and the working methods they use.

There are three elements to the successful new brand, and they run as a constant theme through the whole development programme:

1. It must be salient and relevant to people's needs, wants or desires.
2. It must be a coherent totality.
3. It must be a unique blend of appeals.

1. *It must be salient and relevant to people's needs, wants or desires*
That is, the new brand must stand out from the crowd and it must satisfy the whole range of people's wants in a product type, not merely the functional needs. Consumer appeal is today a fairly standard part of the marketing orthodoxy. Levitt, in his famous article "Marketing Myopia"[1], warns very powerfully against confusing means, which are what most concern manufacturers, and ends, which are really all that interest the consumer deeply. What we need for planning new brands is to get back to basic motivations and human activities; not to be too concerned with the existing means of meeting the needs. And this affects both the way in which objectives are set and all the methods by which the new brand is created and evaluated.

It is by no means an easy principle to put into practice. If the objectives are set too broadly then nothing practical seems to follow. On the other hand, failure to understand that a new brand must satisfy the *full range* of needs and desires can be very expensive. DuPont's Corfam is an example. Corfam was a substitute material for leather, launched by DuPont in 1963 after about thirty years of discussion, research and development. Leather is chemically a very complex material, the structure of whose fibres varies through the thickness of the hide, allowing it to absorb and evaporate moisture. In shoes this gives it qualities of softness, durability and resilience, while it allows the feet to breathe. After a long and troublesome period of bridging the gap between laboratory and production line, DuPont reckoned they had perfected their material. They launched it with the thoroughness to be expected of them—it is said that the brand name was adopted from an original list of 153,000. By all accounts they appear to have marketed it very skilfully. They did not make the mistake of launching a revolutionary *product*. They anticipated competition and launched a revolutionary *brand*. After about four years the competition began to materialize, and even the leather industry was shaken out of its myopia. But Corfam was well established then and seemed set for a huge success.[2]

By 1970, the situation looked rather different. DuPont had not managed to reduce production costs of Corfam a great deal, and thus one of its advantages—smaller wastage in shoemaking—had not been fully exploited. Sales were building up, but simply not fast enough. When DuPont decided in March 1971 to stop production, its cumulative losses were said to be over $80 million—no doubt a world record for a new brand.

[1] LEVITT, T., "Marketing myopia", *Harvard Business Review*, July–August 1960.
[2] GERLACH, J. T., and WAINWRIGHT, C. A., *Successful management of new products*, p. 153 (London, Pitman Publishing, 1970).

The basic cause of failure was probably that it is not yet possible to imitate leather synthetically at an economic cost. But in many ways the real problem with Corfam was that it was not relevant to people's total needs. In most respects Corfam was no better than leather, and it did not take a shine quite as well or adapt itself to the shape of the foot quite as well. In one respect however it was markedly superior: it wore much longer. The question is whether a material that is more expensive than leather but longer lasting represents the real desires of buyers of shoes. What has happened in shoes is that cheaper synthetic materials have been used in increasing quantities, particularly PVC. They have been acceptable partly because women's shoes tend to be more ventilated than men's and do not need the same porous material. But the question of relevance to needs goes much deeper than that, to the very nature of the rewards of shoes. It looks as if DuPont, with all their experience, had concentrated too much on the function of shoes—protection of the feet and comfort for walking. At the non-functional level shoes are clearly much more than this—an intrinsic part of fashion, an expression of one's mood or an extension of one's personality, a status symbol, an accessory, a demonstration of style. Durability is irrelevant to all this. What some people want is traditional style, and Corfam could not challenge leather for them. What others want is cheap, up-to-date, throwaway style. If the product lasts indefinitely and costs a lot, it is a positive embarrassment.

The moral for the new brand is clear. It must come not only from the consumer's needs and wants, but from the *totality* of his needs and wants, functional and non-functional.

2. *The successful new brand must be a coherent totality*

All the evidence makes it clear that a successful new brand must be a totality, not a collection of little bits—however good the individual bits may be. The implications of the retail audit and consumer panel data, those of blind versus named product tests, brand personality research, as well as plain common sense, all suggest strongly that the difference between success and failure lies in the totality of the new brand. People buy brands in shops, not concepts or naked physical products or propositions or attributes or special features.

It is clear too that all the elements of the brand are interrelated. The way a food product tastes depends on the style of the pack, and the way the pack is perceived and appreciated and remembered depends on the taste. If the style of pack of a new brand is changed radically, then the people attracted to it will differ and so will their tastes and price expectations. A change to a higher price is likely to require a more refined physical product and more expensive pack; and so on. It is fairly obvious that all the aspects of a new brand are interrelated;

24

yet all too often we find marketing men trying to test them in isolation or predict the results of varying one element in isolation. Concepts are tested as forms of words; tastes are tested apart from names or packs; packs are tested apart from physical products or prices; names are tested on their own.

Looking at the new brand as a whole certainly presents problems of design, planning and evaluation. But if we do not, we shall end up with something that is an Identikit, not a person.

3. *It must be a unique blend of appeals*

The need for uniqueness hardly needs further stress; it is the difference between the brand and the product. Only if the brand has no adequate substitute, only if it can create a sort of monopoly in the mind of the consumer, will it be able to sustain profits against competition over the years.

The elements to be blended are essentially of two different kinds: physical things and communications—on the one hand, the product and on the other, the name, reputation of manufacturer, pack, styling, advertising, merchandising, word-of-mouth and other associations. The balance differs in different industries. In cosmetics a new brand's communications are of crucial importance and can succeed despite a completely standard set of physical products; in machine tools a good new physical product can overcome mediocre communications. But in any market there must be a blend. It was always a myth about the world beating a path to the door of the man who invents an improved mousetrap.

The way these appeals are blended is less simple and, as Corfam showed, it is easy to miss out some elements. For any new brand the appeals lie in three areas: the senses, the reason, and the emotions.

APPEAL TO THE SENSES
How the brand appeals to the senses of smell, taste, touch, sight or hearing. For instance:

A soup:	its taste; smell; colour, etc.
A floor polish:	its consistency; colour; smell, etc.
A power drill:	its colour; general or surface design; weight and feel in the hand; size; noise when running; ease of use and adjustment; length of cable, etc.

APPEAL TO THE REASON
The appeal of what the brand contains or what it does, the basic functional appeal—its *raison d'être*. For instance:

25

A soup:	its convenience; quality or amount of ingredients; protein content; suitability for, say, old people; low calorie content, etc.
A floor polish:	its value for money; ease in dispensing or using; speed; durability; depth of finish; double action, cleaning and polishing; germicide content, etc.
A power drill:	its speed of drilling; power; adjustability; safety features; range of accessories; guarantee; after-sales service; durability, etc.

APPEAL TO THE EMOTIONS

The appeal of the style and nature and associations of the brand. Appeals to the emotions make up a very large part of the total brand personality, just as they do with people. Our total judgement of people is certainly governed by their looks and by what they do (their appeals to our senses and reason), but perhaps rather more by their style and manner, their house and clothes and friends. For instance:

A soup:	its style of cooking—experimental or plain English; real meal or quick snack; farm house or continental; simple or complex, etc.
A floor polish:	its approach to polishing—hard work that is rewarding in itself or a chore made easy; synthetic or natural; tough or delicate; a powerful workman or an understanding friend, etc.
A power drill:	its approach to work—industrial competence or understanding of the do-it-yourselfer's problems; simple or complicated; rewarding in itself or through its results; stylish or rugged; male or female, etc.

Clearly the appeals in each of these areas affects those in the other two. For instance, the colour of the drill will affect it on the stylish/rugged scale and it may affect people's beliefs about its power. (Levitt[1] quotes the case of a coloured front panel on a $600 piece of electronic equipment that substantially improved the interest shown in it by expert equipment buyers.) It is skill in blending these appeals as much as skill in making individual improvements that leads to success.

There are some solid advantages in analysing the appeals of a new brand in this way. First, it means inevitably looking at the brand from the consumer's point of view; we are less likely to run into problems of irrelevance to people's real wants. Secondly, it helps us to be comprehensive. Thirdly, as will become clear, it is a division of appeals which

[1] LEVITT, T., *The marketing mode*, p. 184 (New York, McGraw-Hill Book Company, 1969).

26

can help to blend the physical product and the communication elements. Fourthly, it relates specifically to different types of consumer research throughout the whole development process.

The Need for Theory

These pages spent on analysis of what makes new brands succeed may seem rather over-theoretical to the manufacturer who simply wants to get on with the job. But in many ways understanding the nature of new brands is the most important part of the whole operation. These three apparently simple requirements for a new brand—its salience and relevance to needs; its totality; its unique blend of appeals to the senses, the reason and the emotions—dominate every decision about organization and every part of the development programme suggested in the rest of this book.

2   *Organizing for New Brands*

$\mathbf{M}$anagement's first task is to establish the company's new brand policy—whether new brands will be developed and, if so, how many. As we have seen, it will depend on the size of the company, but nearly always it will be best to work on a very small number, aiming to establish one major new business every few years rather than half a dozen minor ones every year. The next job is to get the policies carried out, by setting up the right organization, choosing the right people, motivating them and monitoring their progress. This is where it is useful to have analysed the nature of successful new brands, because their nature is what governs how the job of developing them is tackled; and that governs the form of organization, the role of management and methods of control.

WHAT SORT OF WORK IS IT?

Each of the three basic elements of the successful new brand affects the sort of work needed and hence the right sort of organization. To take them in turn:

1. *The successful new brand must be salient and relevant to people's needs, wants or desires.* The obvious implication of this is that the whole direction of the development of the brand must be in the hands of people whose starting point is the consumer and what consumers want. That normally means the marketing men, and on the whole in consumer goods companies it is the marketing men who are in charge of new brands. It is less true of industrial goods companies; it is significant that in the NICB studies[1] the most important single reason

[1] NATIONAL INDUSTRIAL CONFERENCE BOARD, "Why new products fail", *The Conference Board Record*, October 1964.

28

given for new product failure was insufficient knowledge of the market or a complete misjudgement of it.

What is not quite so obvious to marketing men is that running an existing brand and developing a new one are two very different modes of work. The Brand or Product Manager who handles an established brand has in practice surprisingly little freedom of movement. First, he has to work within his budget and this means that anything extra he spends on one element of his total marketing mix has to come off another. He is not normally in a position to create extra funds. His second restriction is often in the distribution mix. In any multi-brand company it is unusual for any single brand to have its own specially designed sales force or distribution system. The brand manager usually has to make the most he can out of a sales/distribution system which is virtually fixed. His greatest freedom of choice comes in the design of his brand, but even here it tends to be restricted. He can, from time to time, improve or reformulate the physical product (indeed he usually must, if the brand is to go on being successful), but it will only be from time to time, and the changes have to be within fairly narrow limits. The price can be manipulated, but within narrow limits and not very often. The design and structure of the pack can be changed, but the need to retain the identity of the brand in the store and in the eyes of the consumer mean that changes must be quite gradual. He can certainly play about with his advertising and consumer promotion expenditure; but again he knows from experience and from generalized marketing knowledge (for instance, the Andrex/Delsey history or Nielsen's analysis of growth brands[1]) that to spend too little is very risky, while to spend too much would be unprofitable. So as often as not the brand manager finds that the element he can change most radically, though again not too frequently, is the style and content of the advertising and promotion and the use of media.

This is not by any means to belittle the job of the brand manager. These modifications to the marketing mix are very important, and can have a great effect on the company's profits. But the fact is that he is operating within very narrow limits. What really controls him is the market-place. The two most crucial elements in consumer buying are more or less fixed in the short term; that is, the *reputation of the brand* and people's *experience of the physical product* in use.

It is all very different with a new brand. There is no existing set of experienced users, no fixed history of use and reputation. All the elements of the brand mix can be varied enormously. And the more a

---

[1] A. C. NIELSEN COMPANY LIMITED, "The marketing wheel—USA, *Nielsen Researcher*, July–August 1968; "Manufacturers' advertised brands", *Nielsen Researcher*, July–August 1970.

new brand gets away from the confines of an established market, the more freedom there will be to vary price too.

With an established brand the brand manager can refine his marketing mix by using an experimental approach. That is, he can hold most parts of the mix constant and test variations in other parts— different promotions or advertising weights or formulations, and so on. But this working method is bound to fail for new brands. The trouble with the new brand is that nothing is fixed; there can be no question of building up from a firm base.

As a result marketing men have often tried to test each of the elements of a new brand in isolation—probably because of the apparent complexity of doing otherwise. (After all, if there were only five main elements to be blended into a new brand and if each of these had only three possible variations, there would still be 243 possible combinations—far too many to test.) Yet common sense and all the evidence tell us that developing a lot of elements separately would be very unlikely indeed to yield a coherent and successful new brand.

The fact is that planning a new brand is a completely different process from running an established one. It is neither a step-by-step deductive process nor a matter of experimenting with extras on a firm base. Planning for new brands starts at the other end. *It starts with the totality and works back towards the elements.*

It is rather like the difference between improving your house and having a new one built. If you want better windows in your house, you can simply experiment with different types until you get what suits you best, from the point of view of aesthetics, price, insulation, durability and so on. Your choice of window will be governed mainly by the period and style of the house as a whole and your income. It is a totally different matter, if you are trying to judge the best windows for a new house. You might make some broad judgements, but until the new house as a whole is conceived (itself a result of analysis of what you want from a house) you cannot possibly get to work on the windows.

It would be quite unfair to suggest that marketing men are not capable of the modes of thought and work processes needed for new brands; that they are intrinsically builders, not architects. But it is true to say that their regular jobs, though using many of the same techniques of consumer research and the same devotion to the consumer and experience of the market-place, are based on a different type of work. And not many people are very good at working in two different ways with the same sort of material at the same time. This consideration must have a fairly fundamental effect on setting up the right organization for developing new brands.

2. *A successful new brand is a totality, a blend of physical product and*

communications. If a new brand is planned in the right way, starting from the totality and working back towards the different elements, the critical part of the job will be blending them and getting the best contribution from each element. The problem is that quite different skills are needed to produce the physical product and the various communications elements, and yet each plays some part in getting each of the desired appeals. For instance, a research chemist might have the skills needed to develop the right odour for a face cream; a production engineer might have the skills needed for producing a fluffy aerated texture; and how it feels on the consumer's face will be affected by the style of the pack and whether it is called Medicated Skin Food or Exotique—the responsibility of pack designer and copywriter. Yet all these are elements in the sensual appeal of the new brand.

There are two very clear organizational implications here. The first is that there must be one person responsible for the new brand, whose main aim is to keep an eye on the totality, while others are developing their individual elements with their individual expertise. There seems no reasonable possibility of ending with a coherent brand unless the end-result is one person's sole responsibility. He will not necessarily be an expert in any one of these specific areas, but he will have to know a good deal about each if he is to become an expert blender.

But it goes rather further than that. The second implication is that developing the new brand must be done on a *project team* basis, not on a division of responsibilities into departmental areas. This is for two reasons. The first is that since practically any variation made in his element by one of the experts will modify the effect of the other elements, produced by the other experts, it is inconceivable that they could produce coherent results in a reasonable time period, if they did not all meet and discuss things and understand each other thoroughly. It is inconceivable that the views and problems of each will not be distorted when they reach the others, if all communication has to go through the man in charge.

The second reason for having a project team is a matter of motivation. People simply do not produce their best unless they see what the final objective is. And they will not see what the objective is, if they are told to confine their activities to process analysis or to speeding up a bottle-filling line or to designing a surface for the pack. Even having the project manager explain the total plan, regularly and articulately (and this is rare), is no substitute for the meeting and discussion and modification of views that happen in a project group. It has been established beyond all possible doubt that properly constituted small groups can achieve far more, far faster, than the sum total of the efforts of the same people working individually. They get to know each other properly; working methods and norms of language and behaviour become established. Their ideas can interact and they can disagree with each other without giving offence. The inhibitions that stifle innovation disappear. People enjoy being members of a project group, and it shows.

Again, the whole concept of project group working—bringing in the people concerned with both physical product and communications right at the beginning and keeping them together—has crucial implications for organization.

3. *The successful new brand is a unique blend of appeals.* Developing a unique new brand is obviously a much more inventive process than most in business. It is more like the creative processes of the artist or novelist; it starts with a blank sheet of paper. It is not a deductive process. The main sources for artistic work are intuition and intro-spection. In the world of "marketing science" these are rather frowned upon as sources of information and decision-making. But that may only be a reaction to a previous tendency to use no other source material than hunch. We must clearly get back to a sensible balance, with intuition and introspection playing their proper part. The other crucial element of inspiration to a great artist or writer is the com-mitment to an idea, a burning desire to express some inner feeling. It must be rare for anything *original* to come from an artist or writer unless he really wants to say something.

But this sort of creation is different, you might say, from what is needed in creating new brands. The artist works to meet his own needs, whereas the new brand must please its customers, not its creators. The invention required is more like that of inventing new scientific pro-cesses. This is perfectly true; it must clearly be more purposive than artistic creation. But the fact is that scientific invention *is* very similar to artistic creation. It is not a matter of patient examination of all the data, logical analysis finally drawing one to the inevitable conclusion. What happens is that someone has a theory and he tries it out. The very selection of the data and the way they are collected and laid out is the result of the theory. There is no such thing as "all the facts", however much managements may call for them as a starting point for develop-ing new brands. The number of "facts" about a market is almost infinite. One particular small boy wishing he could eat half his ice cream and keep the rest is as much a fact as Nielsen's estimate of consumer sales of ice cream through grocers. It might be just as relevant to a new brand. But we cannot possibly tell unless there is some *theory* about a new brand and what sort of thing it might be.

The scientist's theory usually comes from intuition; it is based on a background of knowledge, but does not normally derive directly or deductively from it. The whole history of scientific progress is the story of theories that were tested. The theories were stimulated by observation, but not created by it. The process is what Popper[1] has called "hypothetico-deductive".

Much the same is needed for new brand development. There is a continuous series of theories followed by tests, followed by modified or renewed theories, followed by more tests. They are all based on a general knowledge, and the tests themselves are constantly adding to the knowledge. But the knowledge itself does not create the theories; they have to come from something very like artistic creation. This three-part process of theory, experiment and feedback is quite different from most of the working methods used in marketing and production most of the time.

The operating departments of most large and medium-sized companies are there to perform certain tasks in a fairly routine way; the needs on one day are structurally similar to those on another day. Their aim is to achieve these routines as efficiently as possible. So they tend to work to established rules in a hierarchical way, and managers are judged a great deal by how well their departments stick to the rules. They are far too busy dealing with the orderly running of the machine and with any distractions that might upset it to be able to devote a great deal of time to theories or innovation. The whole operating rationale is the antithesis of the processes of scientific discovery.

And this may go for the company as a whole, curiously enough as a result of embracing too wholeheartedly certain techniques of "management science", which are aimed at quantifying and minimizing risks. Very often the result of operating "scientifically" (in fact, it is the opposite way from the true scientific process), of minimizing risks, of trying to turn every decision into a choice between fixed alternatives rather than an open-ended judgement, of working logically and deductively rather than irrationally and intuitively, is that all innovation is stifled.[2]

These differences in method are partly a result of the transition from small entrepreneur to large-scale business. The entrepreneur is motivated by his desire to give something to the world, just like the artist, and by the hope of material rewards. He is bubbling with ideas and propositions, and deeply committed to his brand. On the other hand, the professional department manager already has a going concern to protect, and he has much less to gain, if the new brand succeeds. He will certainly get esteem and status, but he is unlikely to make a

[1] MEDAWAR, P. B., *Induction and intuition in scientific thought* (London, Methuen, 1969); *The art of the soluble* (London, Methuen, 1967); POPPER, K. R., *The logic of scientific discovery* (London, Hutchinson, 1959).

[2] SCHON, D. A., The Reith lectures, *The Listener*, 19 November–24 December 1970.

fortune. He is almost certainly not as committed to the new brand as the inventor entrepreneur. It is hardly surprising if his whole attitude is more cautious.

In fact, a great many new brands of the most inventive sort started in small companies. Levitt[1] produces an impressive list from the US: The motel business was not started by Hilton or Statler, but by small local entrepreneurs with no experience of the lodgings business. The frozen cake revolution was not brought about by the big bakers, like Ward or National Biscuit, nor by the big frozen food companies, but by a small local baker in Chicago, Sara Lee. It was not RCA or General Electric who created a mass market for transistors, but a remote and tiny company in the geophysical business, now called Texas Instruments. Armstrong Cork and Congoleum–Nairn did not create vinyl flooring to replace linoleum—it was Delaware Floor Products. MGM and Paramount did not invent the TV feature series, but new companies like Four-Star, Revue and Desilu. It was not A & P that started supermarkets, but King Kullen on Long Island and Big Bear in Ohio. And in the UK it was the small family business of Wilkinson who were first to exploit the coated stainless steel razor blade, not the huge international Gillette company (who had patented the coating).

And where new products do emerge successfully from large companies, there is often an entrepreneur in charge—one man who, because of family connections or personal qualities, has established himself so firmly that he can indulge in risks and commitment and intuitive processes.

The story of the Xerox 914 copier is a good example. Xerox planned and developed the model in 1955 and 1956, after many years of research and experiment. The management called in no less than three of the best consulting companies to make independent studies of the market opportunities and potential. Two of them advised against marketing the 914, and one saw the prospect of about 8,000 placements at best reached in the sixth year after launching. Most managements would have given up the project entirely. But the Xerox management was then dominated by Joseph Wilson, and he was well practised at disagreeing with patient logic. He felt that the advent of the Xerox 914 would change the rules of the game. So Xerox went ahead, and he turned out to be right. Placements of the 914 began eventually in 1962 and within three years had reached 80,000.

Apart from these entrepreneurs and big-company entrepreneurial dictators, there are of course many large stratified companies which have been successful in developing new brands. It can be done. But the fact remains that the need for inventive processes is bound to conflict

[1] LEVITT, T., *The marketing mode*, p. 54 (New York, McGraw-Hill Book Company, 1969).

with the need for regular, efficient operating methods. It is a very real dilemma for managements. It would be ridiculous to suggest that the company's methods of working should be geared entirely to developing new brands. At the same time it is fairly clear that routine methods are an ineffective way of developing the sort of new brands that will ensure the profitable future of the business.

What management must do is calculate where these methods overlap, and what sort of organization will allow each to flourish. First of all, its own role.

THE ROLE OF MANAGEMENT

New brands involve the long-term growth of a company and its long-term profits. They relate to the nature and style and diversity of the company in the long run. They usually have a direct bearing on investment in new plant, new management and new skills. They pose questions about organization and motivation in the company. They always involve risk.

There is one thing in common for all these characteristics. They are the province of top management. There are plenty of other people who can deal with short-term problems and who can keep the company on its day-to-day course. It is only top management who can decide what the company is to be and do in the future. The chief executive is probably the only man in a large company who can act entrepreneurially.

Yet it is all too common for management's interest in new brands to be fairly superficial—making speeches about the life-blood of the company and examining with interest the ideas that are put up to it. Actually bringing the new brands to the starting line is delegated far below.

In many ways, commitment is the most vital element in developing a new business; and especially commitment at the highest level. The General Foods failure with Gourmet Foods described in Thomas L. Berg's *Mis-marketing*[1] gives an idea of how important it is.

General Foods are the biggest food company in the world, with many new brand successes. In the middle 1950s they decided to establish a stake in the "fancy foods market", which was a grouping of miscellaneous specialist food products made by a lot of tiny companies and marketed in a lot of devious undisciplined ways. General Foods pointed to the rapid growth in people's use of such delicacies (just as manufacturers do in the UK) and reckoned that their marketing and promotional skills could give them a considerable advantage.

[1] BERG, T. L., *Mis-marketing* (New York, Doubleday & Company Inc., 1970).

35

There were not really all that many problems of production, since many of the fancy foods would be natural products; it would be more a matter of buying and packaging.

In 1957 a new range was launched under the name Gourmet Foods, whose *raison d'être* was that they were selected by the company as "the finest foods from the four corners of the world". The range was designed to cover all parts of a meal, and there were 50 separate items, 18 of them new to the US market. They included products like onion consommé with sherry, champagne mustard, sauce Bolognaise, marinated artichoke shells, Assam tea and cherry pickles. By all accounts, the launch of Gourmet Foods was fairly successful, but repeat-buying was clearly low and sales came to only about $1 million in the first year. There was a rapid change of direction and a new, broader distribution policy, but it seemed to make little difference, and by 1960 the whole range was taken off the market.

It is possible, as it always is in retrospect, to point at all sorts of mistakes and causes of the failure—said to have cost General Foods $3 million. The whole concept may have been wrong; grouping fancy foods together into a category sounds more like manufacturer thinking than consumer thinking. The brand itself was almost certainly not designed properly as a totality, with a clear personality; the very name Gourmet Foods suggests commodity marketing. It was almost certainly a mistake to shift distribution from the specialist shops to the supermarkets without changing any other elements of the mix.

But the real lesson of Gourmet Foods is the importance of top management's role. First, from Berg's account, it seems that the objectives of the exercise were not too clear. Were Gourmet Foods a sort of promotional device for General Foods, to bring them a reputation for really caring for good food? Or was the range meant to be a set of experiments to see which lines could become the next massive food brand? Or were Gourmet Foods expected to be a big profit-earner, and if so, when? Each of the three objectives would have been quite reasonable in itself; what must have been wrong was to hope vaguely that they would all be achieved. In the event it seems that the main objective was prestige, but the measure of achievement was profit. The second point, and maybe a crucial one, was the degree of commitment. An obvious question, which must surely have been discussed frequently, was whether the specialist and fragmented fancy foods market was the right sort of market for a company whose skills lay in production and marketing on a massive scale. Presumably the answer was yes; and yet it seems to have been a rather half-hearted yes. Gourmet Foods were on the market only two and a half years, during which time its total media advertising expenditure totalled only about $2 million. The range was withdrawn at the time when many retailers and some of its own executives believed that it was just starting to move ahead. The end came as a surprise to some of the middle management, who apparently had no clear idea of what would be a break-even point acceptable to the General Foods' Board.

Batchelors' treatment of Vesta dried meals was a complete contrast. The range got off to a fairly bad start. There have always been

FIGURE 7. **How Batchelors recast the personality of their dried meals brand: the original 1960/1 pack and the Vesta pack of 1962**

considerable prejudices against dried foods in the UK, and the quality of the earliest complete meal packs was hardly likely to have dispelled them. The Batchelors name, under which the new range was launched, had been associated almost entirely with processed peas, and that inevitably classed the new range as a little pedestrian. Above all, the personality of the new brand was undoubtedly one of meat-and-two-veg. Instead of withdrawing the range, on the grounds that its sales and profits were rather poor, Batchelors persisted and completely re-cast the brand. The name Vesta was given all the prominence, with Batchelors there simply as company reassurance. The range and its style were redesigned to have a personality of "safe foreign-ness", a sort of traditional British exoticism. Almost immediately the curry meals became the main sellers, with the Chinese meals doing quite well too. The new style seemed to work, and Vesta became a great success. It is an object lesson that sheer commitment to developing a new business could have overcome such an umpromising start.

37

Setting Objectives

Part of the necessary commitment for the chief executive lies in setting the right sort of objectives. That means, in effect, not simply passing on financial objectives to those responsible for new brands. It is not much help to development people merely to be told that the company is looking for new brands that will return 25 per cent on investment. All that means is that the new brands must be good ones.

The objectives must be set in terms of markets, products and people, because it is in these that middle management is expected to be involved. The only point of adding financial criteria is to make clear the company's attitudes to risk, the length and amount of investment that it will accept. There are certain markets that simply could not be entered without a long period of investment, and if the new brand objectives cannot accept a distant break-even point, then there is no point in considering them.

It seems very obvious that one of management's main roles in developing new brands is to lay down a set of objectives, based on the company's corporate strategy. In practice, it does not happen very often. A recent survey[1] of 553 UK companies with a turnover of over £¾ million showed that only one-quarter planned further ahead than three years. One result is that development people are all too often asked in effect to "come up with some ideas and we'll let you know if you're on the right lines". Or, as happened with one major UK company, they were expected to work out the right markets to enter by a deductive whittling-down process, starting with the Gross National Product.

Setting company objectives is a difficult and creative task. In some companies corporate planning has been established as a separate function in the organization, with a member of the board in charge.[2] But, however successful this may be, it cannot absolve the chief executive from the *responsibility* for setting long-term objectives. It is almost certainly best done—as with most creative tasks—by his setting up a project group and leading it himself. The more he can involve in this the people who will be responsible for carrying out the objectives, the better.

Management Style

Beyond setting the company objectives and being committed to them,

[1] HAYHURST, R., MANN, J., SADDIK, S., WILLS, G., *Organizational design for marketing futures* (London, Allen & Unwin, 1972).

[2] STEINER, G. A., "The rise of the corporate planner", *Harvard Business Review*, September–October 1970; THOMAS, D. M. C., "Corporate strategy in a medium-sized company", *Management Decision*, Vol. 9, Winter 1971.

the chief executive has a vital role to play in developing new brands, through setting the management style.

First, he has to make risk-taking and innovation seem rewarding, both in themselves and in their results. He must minimize the company's natural resistance to change. He has to show that different working methods are appropriate to different parts of the organization. In some parts the need is greatest for order, system, planning, checking and control; in others it will be intuition, informality and enthusiasm. He is unlikely to succeed in getting worth-while new brands, unless he delegates fairly permissively and encourages participation. He has to have the vision to appoint a project leader whose management style may be entirely different from his own. He must be ready to drop some of his formal duties at inconvenient times, in order to have rambling inconclusive discussions with his project managers. Once he starts behaving as an authoritative line manager, he will not get consultation or discussion about new brands, but presentations. The project teams will start modifying their plans because of what they think he will say.

Secondly, he has to create an environment in which project groups will work properly. That means that the members of them have to be reasonably well balanced in status as well as in skills. In most companies the departmental structures hardly encourage such balance. On the whole, the marketing men have greater status and higher pay than their opposite numbers on the production side[1]; they have more university graduates and have developed their own language and mysteries—from demand curves to media optimization models. Yet in new brand development the production man's job is often much harder and much more important.

There are the same sort of problems in research and development departments. The fundamental researcher, the pure scientist, tends to have a higher status than the process engineer. All too often R & D departments seem to be split into esoteric boffins on the one hand and obedient but uninspired mechanics on the other, with no means of communication between them. (This may be particularly true of the UK, where roughly three times as many people are trained as scientists as are trained in engineering, though the country's needs are probably the reverse.)

In any company which has these problems of balance and departmental status, it is going to be difficult to set up really productive new brand project groups. The chief executive's management style can make all the difference. He can openly take an interest in all aspects of

[1] HAYHURST, R., MANN, J., SADDIK, S., WILLS, G., *Organizational design for marketing futures* (London, Allen & Unwin, 1972).

39

the company; he can get involved in and promote the "low-status" areas; he can be ready to plan the careers of promising individuals, shifting them from one department to another. Perhaps most important, he can establish informal working relationships as the norm.

Many managements are ready enough to try to create this sort of atmosphere in their companies, provided that it does not interfere with line management authority. They will cultivate friendly relations and Christian names with project managers, provided that they can get clear and quantified reports on progress. They will accept somewhat loose structures for new brand development, as long as there is a clear-cut series of check points for financial decision-taking, with absolutely reliable forecasts. But this is to want it both ways. If the chief executive really wants to develop successful new brands, then he must accept and be committed to informal and innovative working methods.

WHAT SORT OF ORGANIZATION?

The more practical, and probably most important, part of management's job is selecting the right people and setting up the right organization to develop new brands. It seems to be generally agreed that faulty organization is a major cause of failure. Booz, Allen and Hamilton's regular series of surveys[1] of successful new product companies in the US have asked what problems they had, and always difficulties in organization have loomed large. In their most recent report, no less than 81 per cent of these *successful* companies reported problems of organization, more than twice as many as reported any other problem.

Current Practice

There does not seem to be much consistency in current organizational practices, and that may mean that there will be problems, however new brand development is organized. One major survey in the US, carried out by Management Research and Planning Inc.,[2] covered successful major companies in nine industries, including electronics, chemicals, metal fabrication, automotive products and machine tools. The companies were asked which people had new product responsibilities officially assigned to them. Roughly 44 per cent of all the persons mentioned came from technical areas of the company; they were variously described as the New Products Design Section, Forward

---

[1] Booz, ALLEN and HAMILTON, *Management of new products*, 1968.
[2] WARD, A. J., *Measuring, directing and controlling new product development*, p. II–1 (Evanston, Ill., Management Research and Planning Inc., 1968).

Design Section, R & D and Laboratory, and Manufacturing Engineering. About 32 per cent came from the marketing or product manager/ marketing/sales side. In only 12 per cent of cases were staff people responsible, and the usual name for the man in charge was New Products Co-ordinator. In only 2 per cent of cases was a top executive named, including the President; though most companies had a new products committee, whose job might range from screening to total involvement.

On the other hand, the Booz, Allen and Hamilton surveys showed the most common form or organization to be the new product staff department. The proportion of their sample with such departments rose from 22 per cent in 1956 to 86 per cent in 1964. The discrepancy with the Management Research and Planning survey is almost certainly due to the difference between the two samples: "major companies in nine industrial product fields" and "successful new product companies", mainly in consumer goods.

A survey of marketing organization in large companies in the UK[1] emerged with rather less clear-cut answers. This was partly because, when asked the precise title of the executive with the main responsibility for marketing (Chief Marketing Executive), the companies who answered "Marketing Director" or "Marketing Manager" were actually in a minority—34 per cent. In 38 per cent of cases he was called "Sales Director" or "Sales Manager", and in 14 per cent (usually the smaller companies) it was the Managing Director. Thus it was not too easy to interpret findings about full or shared responsibilities for new products. In fact, the survey showed that only 20 per cent of the chief marketing executives had full responsibility for new product planning, but a further 65 per cent had a shared responsibility. Larger companies and consumer goods companies were more likely to give the chief marketing executive full responsibility for planning new products. The survey therefore hinted at some diversity of new brand organization, with the marketing department usually involved. It also suggested that the technical side plays quite a large part and is often given the major responsibility.

One of the problems in seeing how UK companies manage the development of new brands is simply that they have tended to change the system fairly frequently.[2] On the whole, it seems that in the UK at the moment new product departments are rare; the marketing

[1] HAYHURST, R., MANN, J., SADDIK, S., WILLS, G., *Organizational design for marketing futures* (London, Allen & Unwin, 1972).
[2] ACHILLADELIS, B., JERVIS, P., ROBERTSON, A., *A study of success and failure in industrial innovation* (Science Research Council, 1971); LANGRISH, J., GIBBONS, M., EVANS, W. G., JEVONS, F. R., *Wealth from knowledge: a study of innovation in industry* (London, Macmillan, 1972); MORLEY, J. (ed.), *Launching a new product*, p. 5 (London, Business Books Limited, 1968).

department tends to take responsibility in consumer goods industries; R & D tends to be in charge with industrial goods.

Which Department in Charge?

One reason why there is such variety and change is that none of these is ideal. The *marketing department* has a number of advantages. Brand managers develop skills in co-ordination of various specialists. They are more likely than anyone else to start planning from the consumer, and more likely to have some knowledge and understanding of the proper use of consumer research. They are used to dealing with the important communication elements of a brand. They can handle the new brand continuously from the first idea to national marketing, and thus can be deeply involved and committed. On the other hand, there are some fairly serious disadvantages too. First, since the whole process of creating a new brand is fundamentally different from that of running an established brand, the very fact that they look similar superficially could be a very real hidden danger. Secondly, the contact between brand managers and top management is not usually very close; yet it would hardly be possible for the marketing manager or director (who has better contact) to take detailed control of the new brand as well as general control of all the established brands and run his department at the same time. Thirdly, the brand manager may be used to co-ordinating but it is at a relatively routine level, and he may not have the authority or influence to go much further. And finally, the brand manager with an established brand to look after will never be free from short-term problems. His future may well depend on his success or failure with his regular brand. The problem is avoided, of course, if he is working solely on the new brand, but then the brand manager without a going brand tends to have even less authority and contact with top management, and can easily be something of a misfit within the marketing department.

The R & D department has much the same balance, though the advantages seem rather less. Its great asset, especially in product fields where there is a strong technological element, is that it realizes the crucial importance in any brand of the physical product. Not only that, it is in a position actually to change the product, where other departments can merely talk about it. But that is really where the advantages end. Members of the R & D department are not inclined to start with the consumer and do not usually develop much skill in understanding consumer research. They tend to be further than most from the chief executive, who either regards them as backroom boffins or has an exaggerated respect for their technical knowledge. They tend to underestimate or even ignore the values of communication in a new brand.

They tend to be too departmentally committed to do a good job of co-ordination, particularly with outside services.

The new products staff department seems at first much more attractive. By being outside the normal hierarchical line-management system it can have very close contact with the chief executive, and its director—even though he has a very small empire—can be on the company board without disrupting all the other board members' sense of status. It can have complete freedom from short-term problems and departmental vested interests. It can acquire and establish the special skills of developing a new brand. It can be more flexible about the use of outside services. And yet the flaws in giving responsibility for developing new brands to a new products department could be fatal. First, it can very easily get out of the mainstream. It can thereby gradually begin to lack the authority or influence necessary to carry out plans which require the diverse skills of other departments. It may have prestige, through the very idea of innovation and contact with the chief executive, but prestige may not be enough. Secondly, there will be a fatal gap in commitment. If the new brand is to be handed over at some stage to the marketing manager for test or national marketing, who is really responsible for it? The new product staff man cannot really feel the deep commitment that comes from trying out the new brand in the market-place and discovering whether or not it is going to succeed. And the brand manager is taking over someone else's project; if it fails, it is hardly his fault. No amount of getting together and consultations can really get rid of this problem.

Venture Management

The dilemma for the chief executive trying to set up a new brand development organization is clear enough. The organization must clearly draw on the various skills in the company, but it just will not fit in anywhere. It has got to take a marketing approach, but it does not fit happily into the confines of the marketing department. The new brand project group has to have one leader, who has got to work very closely with the chief executive himself; but the chief executive has no department to put him in. If he creates a special one, a new product department, then the whole project may lose touch with the realities of life. The development process has to be a project team process, working by the true scientific method of theory, experiment and feedback; and virtually no other part of the company works that way.

This is why many of the larger companies in the US have tried a completely new approach, which is rather grandly called "venture management". Essentially it is an attempt to create within the company an entrepreneurial enclave.

DuPont have their system of new venture management[1] and Minnesota Mining and Manufacturing have a new business venture division, from which no less than six of its current operating divisions have grown. These two companies were probably the pioneers, but they were rapidly followed by companies like General Mills, Dow Chemicals, Westinghouse, Corning Glass, Monsanto, Celanese and Union Carbide. The essence of the system is that each new project is assigned to a full-time manager, who is given wide responsibilities for developing it, and implicitly the understanding that if it succeeds he will go on managing it. The venture manager of today becomes the divisional manager of tomorrow. Normally he starts off with a small team; gradually, as the project progresses, he calls on more part-time experts and outside resources, until finally the venture, if it looks really promising, takes on the aspect of a small company. The venture manager in a large diversified company is normally responsible to a divisional or departmental general manager; in a small or medium-sized company he is more likely to report to the president.[2] The 3M approach takes the entrepreneurism rather further. The new business ventures division has a budget but no full-time new project managers. The managers are those people in the rest of the 3M organization who have put forward new business proposals which the management of the division thinks are promising—preferably those which result in a product or process which can be patented. Once the project is accepted, the proposer is transferred to the new business ventures division, where he selects his team and manages the project. He gets a first-year budget. His second-year budget will depend more on his skills as a manager and thus the progress made than on the potential profitability of the venture. In the long run, either the project succeeds and the manager becomes head of an operating division; or it fails and he returns to his old division, at least more experienced than he was and having had the opportunity to try out an idea of his own. The very fact that six people have succeeded and become divisional heads, and the risk-taking atmosphere, set by the management style and personality of the company, ensure that there is no shortage of ambitious, entrepreneurial people to submit projects.

There are some very attractive features about venture management. It can start its processes from the consumer, if the new venture manager is essentially a marketing man, without being tied down to the confines of day-to-day marketing work or the responsibilities of an existing brand. It can be entirely committed to the success of the new brand.

[1] PETERSON, R. W., "New venture management in a large company", *Harvard Business Review*, May–June 1967.

[2] HANAN, M., "Corporate growth through venture management", *Harvard Business Review*, January–February 1969.

The venture team is a genuine working project group, and can work in an interacting rather than a departmental way. By being apart from normal divisional operating structures, the team can get a closer contact with top management than it could get within any one department.

But there are certainly problems too. First, there can be a tendency for the top management of the company to play safe. An "entre-preneurial" team is set up, but it really becomes more a microcosm of the existing company, not a facsimile of the founding father's bicycle shop. This is almost bound to happen if the management style of the company is one of efficiency and productivity, and if the new venture is expected to submit to annual plans, cash flow forecasts and budgets.[1] Secondly, most of the new venture management has been based on a *department* or *division*, and it thereby runs into some of the problems of a new products staff department.

A third problem is simply how these people who are entrepreneurial managers are going to emerge. Will a man with, say, experience of running an established brand on the marketing side suddenly for two or three years be able to change his approach and working methods and become an entrepreneur? And what about the other members of the team? If, say, the technical man stays in the new ventures division, will he not get out of touch with the craft of R & D work? Will the market analyst not get out of touch with markets?

However attractive the idea of venture management may be, and however successful it may have been for certain companies, it does not *automatically* solve the basic dilemma of organizing for new brands. There will always be a conflict between entrepreneurism and institu-tionalized systems, but both are necessary for new brands. If new brand project teams are to be genuinely innovative they will have to operate in an environment and style of their own, but one which still manages to make use of departmental skills.

CHOOSING THE RIGHT ORGANIZATION

Clearly the right organization for any company is going to depend on the nature and style of the company, the people in it, technical innovation policy and many other specific factors. But for most com-panies whose policy is to produce the occasional major new brand— that is, occasionally build a new business—these analyses of new brand development work and of current practice tend to point in one direc-tion. The implications are:

[1] LEVITT, T., *The marketing mode*, p. 278 (New York, McGraw-Hill Book Company, 1969); SCHON, D. A., "Champions for radical inventions", *Harvard Business Review*, March–April 1963.

PROJECT MANAGER
One man put firmly in charge of all aspects of the new brand. He should report directly to top management. This will give him the authority to call on diverse skills and people from different parts of the company; and also ensure the interest and commitment of top management. The project manager should probably have been experienced in marketing, though it will be best if he has done other jobs too. He should be explicitly appointed general manager of the new business when it emerges. This will provide him with some of the motivation to be entrepreneurial, and will ensure that he is committed to the new brand from the earliest planning all the way to post-marketing modifications.

This is naturally the key appointment. The project manager's skills of judgement and leadership could make all the difference between success and failure.

PROJECT GROUP
The project group would be made up of experts *temporarily* assigned. That is, they would work full-time on the new project but still belong to their departments. This would ensure that they do not get out of the mainstream. And it would be essential, in order to get the work done; the new product formula has to be produced in the laboratory, even though the R & D man may share an office with the rest of the project group. Later, the members of the project group might return to their departments, stick with the new business or move on to another new project—depending on their individual skills and inclinations.

DEPARTMENT
This complete project team would neither belong to an existing department nor become a new department. It is simply the temporary nucleus of a new business. (Range extensions would, like improvements to going brands, be handled by the marketing department—and this might mean some overlaps.)

A NEW BRAND STAFF MAN
Maybe a senior man as a new brands director, working in a staff capacity. He would advise the project manager on picking his team and on special new brand development skills and techniques. In particular, he would help him establish project group working methods and the process of theory–experiment–feedback; and he could provide continuity of experience in new brands and in the ways of the company. He would also play a major part in helping top management work out the new brand policy, often before a project manager has been appointed. He might have some assistance in gathering and processing information, but he would not have a department; his role would be an

individual one—keeping the company to the right principles of new brand development.

OUTSIDE RESOURCES
The member of the project group representing the communications side of the new brand, which is so critical to the brand's total appeal, will probably come from outside the company—from an advertising agency or new brand consultancy. That is simply because the place where packs and advertising and naming are designed is usually outside the company. Having an outsider in the project group can bring extra stresses, but has advantages. The communications man will be far less departmentally minded, and will be used to working in project groups and to theory–experiment–feedback methods; he could be a very valuable catalyst.

PEOPLE
The particular skills represented on the project group will depend on the nature of the markets chosen and the likely technological content of the new brand. The project manager may need or want to change its

Project group for developing new brands

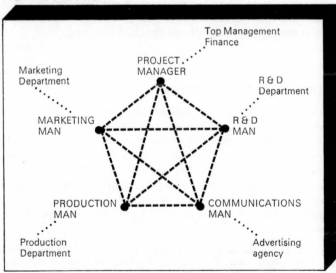

FIGURE 8. The basis of the new brand project group: a project manager, directly linked with top management, and temporarily assigned specialists who can also act as project managers within their departments

constitution as the work develops. In most cases there will be an R & D man, a production man, a marketing man and a communications man in the group; maybe a cost accountant, maybe not. It is a matter of deciding how many people are needed at each stage and which skills are continuously needed through the operation, which are occasionally valuable.

In many ways personal qualities are more important than technical skills. Project group members not only have to have ideas and work well with the others; they also have to be able to get things done, back in their own departments. Working together in the project group will quickly enough broaden their understanding and sympathy for others' problems; but the whole thing will fail if, say, the R & D man cannot get good work out of the laboratory or the communications man out of the agency. Project group members clearly cannot be departmental managers, but they must have managerial skills. They will be acting as project leaders themselves in their own departments.

This can be particularly critical in the R & D department, which may have the hardest job. There have been many diagnoses of the problem of unproductive R & D[1] and there are some common symptoms: too many things done at once, indiscriminately; obstinate refusals to drop a project; jargon; elaborate departmental routines; outsiders greeted with suspicion or dismissed as fools; "mousetrap myopia" (the view that a "better" product inevitably creates its own demand). The R & D man on the project group may well need special help from the project manager and the chief executive.

CONTROL AND EVALUATION

This form of organization may sound a little expensive; there are two very senior people as new brands director and project leader, and three or four senior enough to have managerial skills as full-time members of the project group, plus a fee to the outside communications man. It is expensive, but the costs are likely to be a lot less than an endless stream of new brand failures or, maybe worse, new brands that survive weakly for several years. At least, they seem more reasonable if the operation is looked on as building a new long-term business.

[1] COOK, L. G., "How to make R & D more productive", *Harvard Business Review*, July–August 1966; EILOART, T., "Fanning the flame of innovation", *New Scientist*, 11 September 1969; HANAN, M., *The market orientation of R & D* (American Management Association, 1965); MUSE, W. V., and KEGERREIS, R. J., "Technological innovation and marketing management", *Journal of Marketing*, October 1969.

Company management simply has to decide whether it is going to take new brand development seriously or not. If it is, then it must pay the cost of having a proper organization to do it.

Another of the prices to be paid for effective innovation may have to be the abandonment of the control methods that the chief executive finds most useful in running the rest of the business.

A Flexible Approach

The reason for a more flexible approach to control of new brand development is fairly simple. Normal control methods can be used for range extensions and product improvement for going brands, because on the whole they are step-by-step deductive processes; because they are usually experimenting with one or two elements only; and because the brand manager normally has a good idea of what the end result will be. It is not too hard to predict the time and costs likely to be involved. Estimates of the return on investment are not likely to be far out, because they are essentially modifications of known data.

None of this is true for the new brand. The whole point of the theory–experiment–feedback method is that no one knows the results before the work is done. The project manager is not varying one or two elements in a known mix; he is trying to create something entirely new. Usually it is a matter of a few false starts and several modifications before the new brand reaches the critical point of appeal to consumers. It may be possible to predict reasonably accurately the timing and cost of each stage of the process immediately before it starts; what is very difficult is to predict how many stages there will be or the cost of the stage after next.

The development programme set out in the rest of this book takes the new brand gradually from being a tentative idea to being a solid entity whose performance in the market-place is reasonably predictable. Thus in the later stages of the programme it behaves much more like an established brand and is much more subject to normal controls. Fortunately the more informal and creative stages of the programme are considerably cheaper than the later stages, and they are usually quicker too. The longest tests of the new brand are those that take place when it is near to its final form.

Usually it is the timing that worries managements most. All too often the need for a major new brand is not really pressed until the marketing situation for the established brands has become rather difficult; profits and cash flow are beginning to be a worry. Then the demand is for a profitable major new brand to be developed extremely quickly, without wasting any money on unnecessary research. The programme must be laid down and kept to, whatever the research

49

findings. The critical date is the launching date for the new brand; everything must fit in with that. It is an absolutely sure-fire formula for failure.

Most of the textbooks emphasize the importance of timing for the success of a new brand. Most manufacturers are deeply affected by the idea of competitors getting in first. The finance men are constantly harping on the need for new brands to move rapidly from the cost-incurring development stage to the profit-earning stage of national marketing—usually on the basis that the new brand will inevitably have a short life (the naïve life-cycle theory), and a lengthy development stage could eat into this life or at least postpone the payback year.

There is something in these arguments, and timing is occasionally very critical. It is most likely to be so in expensive products where styling is important and technological change rapid—cars, for instance (though it is hard to imagine that timing was critical for the original Volkswagen beetle). But for the most part the importance of precise timing is rather a myth, and to some extent a self-fulfilling myth. Clearly any successful new brand must be in tune with current trends, but it is usually a matter of introducing it in the right year, not the right month. It can only very rarely be worth cutting out development stages or hurrying them too fast, to save time. The object is to build up a new business which will last a long time, and saving a few months in the development stage could be a very false economy.

This is not to say that new brand development does not need careful control and evaluation by management. It is not so much the type of controls used as *how* they should be used, *by whom* and *when*. The two most useful techniques—critical path analysis and return on investment calculations—are conventional enough, but they have to be used with great care.

Critical Path Analysis

Critical path analysis (or network analysis) is an obvious method for programming development processes. It has many advantages in the later stages (which are described on p. 149). But it does have some dangers in the earlier, more creative stages. First, the very fact that it breaks down tasks into departmental operations can actually destroy the cohesion of a project group. Each member concentrates on his own task and the time allotted to it (always too little, compared with the others' allotments) rather than to the tasks of the group as a whole. Secondly, the problem of predicting the time needed for any task is much harder in the earlier stages, and there is a great temptation to play safe; so that the total operation can actually take longer than it would have done without network analysis. The third danger is the greatest. Critical path analysis can become such an attractive toy that it takes over the whole development process, and timing becomes more important than getting the new brand absolutely right.

On the whole, it is usually best to use simple calendar schedules for the early stages, bringing in network analysis only at the stage of preparing for the market-place. And even there it is often best that it should be seen as an internal means of controlling progress for the project group, rather than a weapon for outside management.

Financial Controls

Financial calculations are needed to deal both with budgeting for development costs and with choosing between alternatives or making go/no-go decisions. The calculations get gradually more critical as the project progresses, but essentially what is needed then is more judgement and entrepreneurism, rather than more statistical techniques. It is not hard to work out the basic salary budget for the project team. It is less easy to predict early capital requirements—pilot plant or even laboratory equipment. Again, this is because there cannot, in proper new brand processes, be any very clear idea of what will be needed beyond each stage. Again, fortunately the early stages tend to be a lot less demanding, and could normally be dealt with by allocating the project team a contingency budget.

However, the time ultimately comes when the company must face heavy expenditure in plant or equipment or people. In the biggest companies there may possibly be problems of choice between two competing project teams. There could be questions of choosing between investment in new plant for an established brand and investment in the new brand. But on the whole such choices must be made on the basis of company policy; if the decision has been made to develop a new business, the choice may be irrelevant. Comparing new brand investment with normal investment decisions can be very misleading; it is not helped very much by allocating probabilities in order to deal with the element of risk. And the choice between alternative new brands, where they are of entirely different types, should be much more dependent on what the company reckons it is good at doing and what it wants to do than on a predicted rate of return.

The fact is that predictions of return on investment (quite apart from the various interpretations of the term) for new brands can be wildly inaccurate. It is very easy to be misled because a standard control measure—return on investment—is clearly the best sort of measure for decisions about new brands. Other things being equal, the use of discounted cash flow with return on investment calculations is a valuable refinement.[1] But there is something ludicrous about worrying whether the discount rate should be 8 per cent or 9 per cent for year 10, when predictions of sales and profit margins for year 1 could be 300 per cent out.

Return on investment calculations for new brands are just as double-edged as network analysis, in much the same sort of way. They can give a false aura of certainty to something whose outcome is entirely uncertain, and deceive people into making decisions that under normal conditions of uncertainty—that is, using intuition and judgement—they would never make. Any attempt to tie the project manager to detailed forecasts could either produce figures that are designed to be acceptable rather than realistic[2] or, maybe worse, induce a degree of caution that finally kills the spirit of enterprise and the new brand's chance of success.

Again, there must be a sense of proportion. It is not necessary, in order to avoid the dangers of over-control in financial predictions, to ignore profitability altogether. What is needed is a series of very rough predictions, of a back-of-envelope type not a discounted-cash-flow type, as the whole programme proceeds. Gradually these predictions can become more firm and more elaborate. By the time a pilot market or test market is analysed it would be reasonable to use the full processes.

Internal Control

What this means is that, during most of the new brand development programme, the chief executive will not have the same sort of control information as he sees for his going brands. In fact he will have a different sort of control for new brands, and provided that he has chosen the right project manager and set up the right sort of organization and methods and motivation, it will work much better. And that is the internal control of the project team itself. Its own determination to succeed, its commitment to the new brand and, for the project manager, the realization that the new brand is not just an abstract creation but a management career for himself; all these will be much better disciplines to encourage reasonable speed and reasonable potential profits than external controls.

[1] BLACK, M., "DCF values new product investment", *Advertising Management*, March 1970; GABOR, A., "Marketing's role in investment decisions", *Marketing*, September 1970; SCHEUBLE, P. A., "ROI for new product policy", *Harvard Business Review*, November–December 1964; WELTER, P., "Put policy first in DCF analysis", *Harvard Business Review*, January–February 1970; WINER, L., "A profit-oriented decision system", *Journal of Marketing*, January 1966.
[2] POLLITT, S., "A practical approach to new products and new concepts", *Admap*, March 1970.

Control and evaluation is as much a matter of management style as of specific technique. And like so many of the ingredients of success with new brands it comes back to underlining what new brands are, what processes are needed to produce them, having a policy and motivating the right people. The project team needs not only to be set up in an entrepreneurial way, but to have entrepreneurial faith behind it.

Apart from this internal control, the chief executive can more conventionally monitor progress by establishing a fairly standard *new brand development programme*. His own involvement, once the programme is established, can be as a sympathetic audience for progress achieved within it, not as a rigid controller of funds and creativity.

The rest of the book is about the design of this programme.

3   A New Brand Development Programme

The new brand development programme illustrated here aims to provide a balance between the need for careful planning, control of progress and integration of work and the need for creative freedom and theory–experiment–feedback methods. The next three chapters deal with each of the stages in turn.

The three stages are called *planning*, *development* and *evaluation*. They represent a gradual refining of ideas and bringing them to physical form; and a gradual move from total uncertainty towards a reasonable predictability. The stages do of course blend into each other, and it is never easy to draw lines between them. But it is still helpful to look at them as three separate stages, since at the end of each one there is a natural stopping-point, at which the whole project can be reviewed. The review is both by the project team and by top management. Unless the project team sets itself the discipline of considering progress in a formal way at set points it can easily be led too far in directions that are not quite right, through its own enthusiasm and commitment. Equally it is best for top management to review progress formally at set points—even though the evaluation measures will sometimes be very primitive—rather than constantly peering over the project team's shoulders.

These stages also represent increasing amounts of time and money. Implicit in the review at the end of each stage is the decision to budget more time and money than has been spent so far. Even though it may be sensible, from the point of view of motivation, for the chief executive to allow the project manager to make the decision, he will certainly want to see that it is a carefully-taken decision, not simply an emotional desire to go on. It is undoubtedly depressing to have to go right back to the beginning at the end of the first or second stage. But it is a great deal

Planning stage

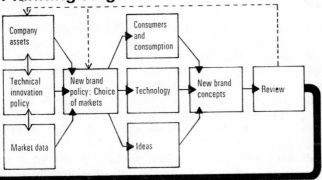

Development stage

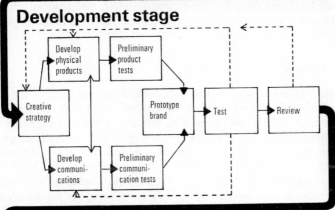

Evaluation stage

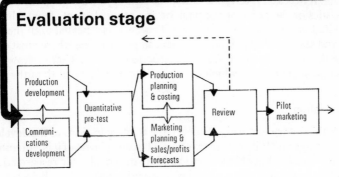

FIGURE 9

55

more depressing and it can be destructively expensive to start again after a failure at the end of the third stage.

Planning

The planning stage starts with analysis of the company's new brand policy, its strengths and weaknesses and possible areas for developing a new business. This leads to the choice of a market, or a small number of markets. When this choice has been agreed by management, the project team studies the present and likely future technology, market structure, consumer behaviour and attitudes in the market. They can also use formal methods to search for ideas and various devices to stimulate their own skills in innovation. The end of all this is a number of new brand ideas—loose theories about the sort of new brands that might be successful and might fit in with the company's skills, policies and style. These ideas are then broadly and open-mindedly screened against the original objectives and financial criteria; and the company's objectives are reviewed in the light of these specific propositions.

Development

More detailed objectives are then worked out for each of the new brand ideas, in terms of a proposed synthesis of appeals to the senses, the reason and the emotions. This creative strategy then becomes a preliminary design brief for the whole project team; it is the means of integrating all the elements of the new brand. The physical product and the communication elements are then created to this brief, and they are each crudely tested on their own, before being put together as the *prototype new brand*. This is itself tested, and the results are fed back, if necessary, to refine either the strategy or the physical characteristics or the name or the pack or any other element; from which a revised brand emerges for testing. This cycle is repeated until the new brand seems right. This development stage is the one where most of all the theory–experiment–feedback process operates. There follows the second stage review, which can be a little more refined than the first.

Evaluation

The third stage is a bridge between the pilot operations of the development stage and full-scale marketing. The central part of it is a quantitative pre-test, whose aims are to validate the small-scale research done so far, to try out a few experimental variations and to help set the right pricing policy. After this, the programme merges into the normal work of the production and marketing departments, as plans are worked out for launching the new brand. Then, after a final review, pilot marketing offers a further opportunity for modifying elements of the brand and for deciding whether it really does provide the basis for a successful new business.

The flow chart shown here is very simplified indeed, and could be a little misleading from two points of view. First, it looks as if only one theory and only one total new brand is developed. Of course there can be, and probably should be, alternatives at each stage. Secondly, it is not possible to produce a readable flow chart which illustrates all the instances of feedback; the whole chart would be covered with arrows and spirals. Just as tests of the total new brand are used to refine the creative strategy, so can practically any test or any piece of information or any idea be used to refine or add to the company's objectives. Indeed the company's objectives can hardly be worked out in practical detail unless there is some of this feedback. In any system like this, where the aim is to produce a unique integrated totality from diverse elements, there should in reality be a line of communication between every process and every other process, just as there should be between each person involved.

The chief executive's main area of *formal* control ends with the establishment of this broad programme of development and his own participation in the reviews at the end of each stage. His contribution *informally* as an involved sympathizer and his commitment to the decisions taken at each stage are likely to be vital to success. But from this point on, how the programme is carried out and what work is done, with what results, will be the responsibility of the project manager.

5

4   *Planning*

The new brand project group has now been set up, and Fig. 10 shows the first stage of its work—originating new brand ideas and picking a very small number of them for further development.

The inputs that go into the project group and help its members crystallize their ideas are put into neat and separate little boxes here, for reasons of clarity. Life is not quite so neat; everything is inter-related. Company policy depends on both analyses of markets and technological forecasts. Ideas depend on technology and so do likely consumer desires; nobody wanted a car in the eighteenth century, and few people want a videophone now. Technology will itself depend on changing social patterns, and certainly any company's development of technology will depend on its own style and policies. And so on.

In the same sort of way, it would be wrong to suggest that each member of the project team is solely responsible for one of the boxes. On the whole, the marketing expert will contribute most to the analysis of market data, the R & D and production men to technology, the communications man to the ideas search. But the whole point of project group working is that each member should contribute to each area as much as he can. It soon becomes clear that, since common sense plays a major part in each skill and since all have been learning indirectly about the other sides of the business during their working lives, the overlap will be quite considerable. Not only that; they will find that a freshness of thought and an ignorance of the problems in any area can often be the key to a totally new and successful approach. The R & D man will often have a crazy idea about marketing which will turn out to work; it will have come from his own intuition and

Planning stage

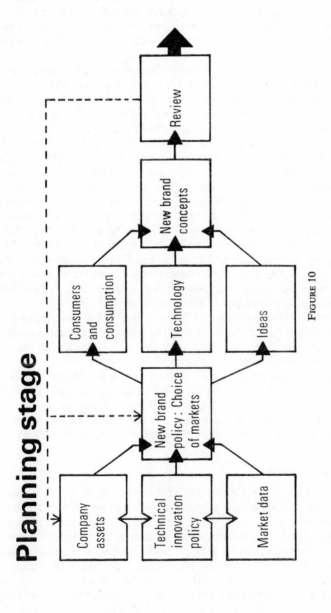

FIGURE 10

introspection as a consumer, whereas the marketing man has discounted his own feelings and relied on consumer research. The sample of one must sometimes be right. Equally, when the marketing man has innocently asked "Why couldn't it be made that way?", the discipline for the R & D man of explaining exactly why it could not is often enough to reveal to everyone that it could. One reason why entrepreneurs succeed with new brands is that in one man these traditional departmental barriers cannot exist. For instance, the success of G-Plan in the late 1950s owed much to the fact that Donald Gomme had particular skills not only as a designer but also as a furniture technologist, production man and marketing man.

The most critical decision for the chief executive and the project manager is the choice of markets to enter with a new brand. What sort of new business does the company want to build up and in what sort of consumer area or product type? The answer will depend on several factors. First, what the company's current resources are; its physical resources, skills, strengths and weaknesses. Secondly, what its strengths and weaknesses might be in the future. Thirdly, what its attitudes to risk and innovation are, how much effort and time is likely to be put into technological development. Fourthly, and in view of the crucial importance of top management commitment to new brands, maybe as vital as any, what the company actually *wants* to do. Finally, trends and opportunities in the markets themselves.

None of these questions is easy to answer. All are subject to modification through feedback. One of the reasons why it often seems so difficult to set company objectives is that managements feel that they must get to the final conclusions in one mighty leap and that the conclusions must then be engraved in stone, to provide the basis for all future action. But this is to use a deductive approach to planning; it would indeed be a very difficult, worrying and responsible task to set company objectives, if this were so. In fact, taken stage by stage with the results considered as working hypotheses, it is not really very hard.

Company Assets

The starting-point then is an analysis of the company's existing strengths, followed by a judgement of where they might lead; and of weaknesses, to look at what areas might be opened up through improvements. It is important that all areas of the company's resources should be considered—R & D, production, plant, raw materials, trade customers and distribution, reputation and links with consumers, finance and so on. In each of these areas the company may have a skill which is relevant to a new brand. The principle is that no company is likely to be particularly successful in developing a new brand or entering a new market without some firm base in production or marketing or finance. It *could* happen that a company would succeed in learning a new technology for producing a new brand in a new market for sale to new customers through new distribution channels, but it is certainly lengthening the odds against it to try to do so. Normally the best policy is to start from some position of strength.

The arguments of "Marketing Myopia"[1] are so powerful that sometimes marketing men have interpreted them too narrowly, and have believed that the starting-point for new brands should always be the markets or consumers' activities. Product-orientation is a rather severe accusation. In theory, this is true enough. In the long run, the company should certainly think of itself as satisfying certain sets of consumer needs. In practice, however, and in the medium term, it seems unnecessarily restrictive to rule out development from the base of existing production skills, if they are a potential source of competitive strength. New production methods are usually much harder to develop and learn than new marketing methods or new consumer habits. And in the end the most vital element in a new brand is a physical product that works at least as well as the best of its competitors. The starting-point for new brands can be from any of the company's assets.

The first thing to do therefore is to list the company's operating strengths in plant, equipment, people, skills, cash, contacts and so on. For instance, under the heading of *Production* there would be:

> plant—types, ages, capacity, flexibility, etc.
> replacement plant—what new capacities?
> production techniques used
> manual skills
> quality control
> management strength and skills
> knowledge of other processes and raw materials
> factory space, seasonal capacity, etc.
> any patents held
> raw materials—buying power and skills, and so on.

Under *Marketing* there would be customers, trade goodwill, contacts, distribution, transport, sales force people and skills, experience in marketing branded goods, advertising, packaging, merchandising, consumer research, knowledge of special techniques (e.g. mail order), management skills.

Then for *Relations with consumers*—including direct experience or

[1] LEVITT, T., "Marketing myopia", *Harvard Business Review*, July–August 1960.

research knowledge about the structure of consumption, people's behaviour and motivations; and, most important, company and brand reputations—their extent, their coverage and their meaning.

Finally, for *Finance*—including company assets, long-term debt, liquidity, cash flow, access to capital, share price, vulnerability to take-over, management skills.

Research and development strengths might be added to the list, but since their implications are usually long-term, rather than operational, it is usually better to deal with them separately—as is done here, under technological policy, on page 70.

Making such lists ought to be quite easy for any company, and it may be because it seems so simple-minded that it is so rarely done. The very act of writing it all down can often surprise the management of a company, particularly if there is a serious attempt to take an objective view of strengths and weaknesses. The best way to be objective about it is to think of each asset in relation to competitors—that is manufacturers in any field who use the same asset; all strengths and weaknesses are relative. It is not that managements are unaware of what is going on in their companies; it is just that they do not very often write all their strengths and weaknesses down on one piece of paper. And they do not often start developing a new brand in this way. It is so much more attractive to say "Frozen food (or cassette TV) will be a great growth market; we ought to have a look at it".

Getting from the current situation to the desired policy is of course not a straightforward matter. Here, as elsewhere, it is a matter of developing a theory, testing it, feeding back information, adapting the theory and so on. The current strengths are at least the firmest starting-point. Another possible starting-point is what the management wants to do; but that is often harder to discover and it can lead rather more quickly up blind alleys.

To see how the analysis of assets is done, let us take a hypothetical case—a manufacturer of upholstered furniture. So far he has listed his assets and roughly evaluated them as strengths or weaknesses. His next stage is to work out, again roughly, where the strengths *might* take the company, at one stage of development. This is based on the idea of the company growing in a series of interlinked chains, always starting from an area of current strength. As soon as the next link in the chain is established, that opens up further possibilities. For instance, a new market entered on the basis of existing production strengths might automatically develop new distribution skills. In this way the company can, on paper, plan several stages ahead. The second move can develop either from the first or be a parallel move from another of the company's current strengths.

The upholstered furniture manufacturer will therefore end up with a series of possible areas for new brands. First, the implication of production assets—that is, where his knowledge and skills in processes, plant and raw materials might lead:

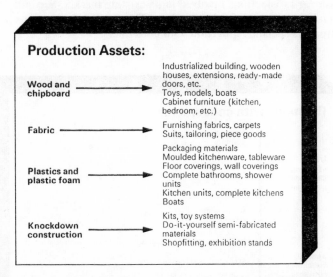

Production Assets:

Wood and chipboard → Industrialized building, wooden houses, extensions, ready-made doors, etc.
Toys, models, boats
Cabinet furniture (kitchen, bedroom, etc.)

Fabric → Furnishing fabrics, carpets
Suits, tailoring, piece goods

Plastics and plastic foam → Packaging materials
Moulded kitchenware, tableware
Floor coverings, wall coverings
Complete bathrooms, shower units
Kitchen units, complete kitchens
Boats

Knockdown construction → Kits, toy systems
Do-it-yourself semi-fabricated materials
Shopfitting, exhibition stands

Then, marketing assets. What sort of business might provide a further outlet for the company's contacts, skills and resources?

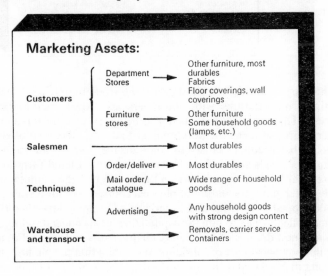

Marketing Assets:

Customers {
Department Stores → Other furniture, most durables
Fabrics
Floor coverings, wall coverings

Furniture stores → Other furniture
Some household goods (lamps, etc.)
}

Salesmen → Most durables

Techniques {
Order/deliver → Most durables

Mail order/ catalogue → Wide range of household goods

Advertising → Any household goods with strong design content
}

Warehouse and transport → Removals, carrier service
Containers

63

Next, the implication of the company's relations with its consumers. There are usually three starting-points for this analysis. First, the understanding that the company has built up of the *full range* of consumer satisfactions involved in its existing market. Secondly, any special contacts with final consumers. Thirdly, the implications of the company's specific reputation with consumers.

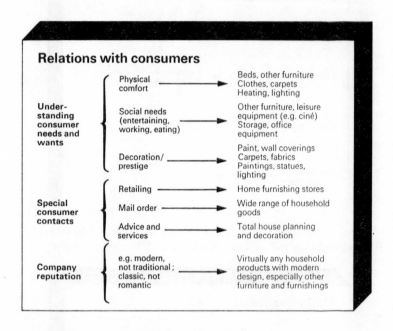

This particular analysis shows both the strength and weakness of starting from relations with consumers, as "Marketing Myopia" suggests. The strength is that, as well as being less myopic, it is a much richer source of ideas for development than the other two areas of assets. Most products satisfy to some degree a very wide range of consumers' needs and desires. For instance, upholstered furniture at the sensual level offers comfort and relaxation. If the manufacturer really understands the nature of physical comfort—if, for instance, he has developed knowledge and experience of ergonomics—then there are many fields open to him for capitalizing on his understanding: for instance, new designs of beds, office chairs, baths and so on. Equally, he will know what sort of fabric/foam combination people find most relaxing in a sofa, and this might lead to a special sort of clothes or bedding or carpets. At the emotional level upholstered furniture

64

satisfies many other wants—our aesthetic pleasures in a room arrangement, our ways of expressing ourselves to friends, our ways of establishing a social group (there is a great difference in the relationships of a group when it is sitting on hard chairs and when it is sitting on upholstered chairs). These social and physical desires are so fundamental that a vast number of possibilities is opened to the manufacturer who understands them deeply. The danger of aiming to develop solely from production skills is that all these possibilities may simply never arise.

The weakness of trying to develop solely from the consumer is simply that the range of options is too great, and it does not *by itself* give the manufacturer a clear line of direction. To take Levitt's best-known example, the US railroads should certainly have thought of themselves as in "transportation". But that alone would not have helped them to make a choice between cars, aircraft, ships, travel services, packaged holidays, escalators, bicycles, moon-rockets and shoes.

The answer is, of course, that if he looks at the implications of assets in all three areas—production, marketing and relations with the consumer—the manufacturer can get the benefits of both the limited view and the completely open view.

The final area of assets—financial—is rather different from the others, in that usually nothing very positive comes from them. But they do set the practical limits. What the company can do to develop at all will depend on how sound it is financially and how good the financial management is, what the current resources are and how liquid they are, what sort of access there is to capital, what the share price and the price/earnings ratio are, and how vulnerable the company may be to a takeover. Though this analysis may be a little negative, it can reveal particularly clearly a crucial part of new brand policy—the company's attitude to risk and its length of vision. A company, for instance, that fears a takeover bid or has strict short-term profit targets imposed by a parent company may well be emotionally unable to get involved in any high-risk activity or one that would require a long investment. This would probably lead to a policy of relatively unambitious new brands which were not very much more demanding than line extensions; that is, very closely related to the current product field. On the other hand, a relatively secure company with large liquid assets but too dependent on one product field (for instance, a tobacco company) might want to aim for high long-term rewards and thus accept high risk and long investments.

There is certainly enough material emerging from these simple analyses to stimulate the project group and top management into thinking what sort of new business it wants. Company policy will itself always be developing, as new information is received and experiments are carried out, but it ought to be possible to give a first broad indication at this stage. It may well be that whole areas can be immediately ruled out. The furniture manufacturer, for instance, may decide that he simply could not envisage his company going into retailing—though he might never have thought of saying so if he had simply been asked what the policy of his company was. This sort of narrowing down of the areas of search can in this way be carried out long before there is any real expenditure of time, money or personal commitment.

TECHNICAL INNOVATION POLICY

The possibilities are narrowed down further by the company's technical innovation policy. Again, this policy has a very critical effect on what sort of new business can be developed, but it is not likely to exist in any precise statement, ready and waiting for the project manager. He has to establish it by discussion with top management, from an analysis of what the company's R & D facility can do immediately and what it might do in future, what sort of technical style the company wants to have and what it is prepared to pay for. Research and development skills tend to change only slowly and they are not easy to build up in the short term; so the current situation has to be assessed very realistically.

For some companies the technical innovation policy emerges very quickly; they simply do not have the resources for any sort of fundamental research or product innovation. Often the R & D department is little more than a polite name for a few quality control technicians. This immediately limits the final choice of markets. In some markets—many food products, for instance—fundamental research is so expensive and problematic in outcome, compared with development work of the trial-and-error type, that very few companies are involved in it; there are still many opportunities for the company with a very limited technical innovation policy. By contrast, it would hardly be feasible for such a company to go into electronic products or pharmaceuticals.

Four Strategies

For other companies, the choice is more subtle. There are four fairly distinct strategies that could be adopted—these are more or less the four picked out by Ansoff and Stewart[1], but three of them are renamed here—pioneer; improver; segmenter; me-too.

PIONEER

The idea of being the first to market a new product type, a pioneer, is certainly a very attractive one. It clearly motivates many of the top managements in many large companies. It is of course the most overtly risky policy, as Rolls-Royce discovered with their use of carbon fibres in the RB 211 engine, and it demands the highest investment in all stages of R & D. But it is likely to be the most rewarding, when it works, and the pioneering advantage can last for many years.[2]

Although it is usually a big company policy, it is quite possible for a small company deliberately to take up a pioneering technical strategy. For instance, Geophysical Services had been operating some sixteen years, specializing in reflection seismographs and oil exploration, and had reached sales of only $2 million, when it changed its name to Texas Instruments and decided to concentrate on pioneering. Twenty-five years later, in 1970, as a result of pioneering such products as silicon transistors, infra-red transmitting glass and semi-conductor integrated circuits, its sales were over $800 million.

It is not really possible to say whether Texas Instruments "invented" the transistor or whether the company built on the inventions of others. And it does not really matter very much. This policy is as much an attitude of mind and a marshalling of resources as a rigid definition. It is a matter of deciding to be the first to exploit or develop something to make it a commercial success.

IMPROVER

A less ambitious strategy is to try to be second in the field with a new product type; it is less risky, but potentially less rewarding. The advantages are that some of the education of customers and final consumers will have been done by the pioneer and many of the mistakes will have been made by the pioneer. The chances of the pioneer getting the product absolutely right first time are not usually very high, and it is easier and very much cheaper to concentrate on improving something that already exists than to invent something that does not. Levitt[3] calls this "reverse R & D", and suggests that it is the right policy for most companies.

---

[1] ANSOFF, H. I., and STEWART, J. M., "Strategies for a technology-based business", *Harvard Business Review*, November–December 1967.

[2] A. C. NIELSEN COMPANY LIMITED, "Seven keys to a strong consumer franchise", *Nielsen Researcher*, May–June 1962.

[3] LEVITT, T., *The marketing mode*, p. 57 (New York, McGraw-Hill Book Company, 1969).

However, it seems questionable whether one can ever learn quite as much from other people's mistakes as from one's own, and the danger is that the pioneer will always stay one technical step in front. At the same time, the company with an improver strategy will still need a fairly heavy expenditure on R & D in order to understand quickly enough the nature of the pioneer competitor's innovations, and to produce a significant improvement on them. The improvement can be in performance or processes or cost, but unless it is noticeable there is no real advantage over the me-too strategy. In addition, only significant improvements will overcome the risk of being blocked by patents.

In other words, the improver strategy, which is likely to be the one chosen by most companies, constantly runs the risk of falling between two stools—getting none of the advantages of the pioneer but costing more than straightforward copying.

SEGMENTER

A third strategy is based on modifying products to meet the needs of particular customers or market segments. (Ansoff and Stewart call it "applications engineering".) It assumes, reasonably enough, that the pioneer will leave specialist gaps, as he steers a middle course and aims to satisfy most of the needs of most of his customers.

The company with a segmenter strategy has the advantage of not competing head-on with the pioneer and the improver, and thus may be able to get a higher margin for his product. But the disadvantages outweigh this as a new brand policy for all but the smallest companies. Even where the pioneer has left a reasonably large gap, he may well be in a good position to fill it later with a range extension. And the segmenter will still have fairly high R & D costs. He will need very good information sources about customers' special needs, and the design and engineering resources to meet those special needs.

ME-TOO

Finally, there is the simple policy of doing practically no technical innovation at all, waiting for others to innovate and then copying them. It is obviously much cheaper in R & D costs.

But it is hard to envisage this strategy working for new brands. It could no doubt produce an occasional success—Babycham, for instance, was not based on a new product; and the importance of technical development is usually over-stressed. But so negative a strategy seems unlikely to succeed very often; and the me-too manu-facturer is increasingly likely to be undercut by retailers' brands. The me-too technical strategy is precisely what is followed by private label products.

Implications for New Brand Development

Thus it normally comes down to a decision whether the company is to be a technical pioneer or a technical improver; or rather, since these clearly cannot be rigid categories, where the company currently stands on the continuum between them. It is an important decision, because it affects the whole way in which new brand development is tackled. It can be fatal to try to develop a new business requiring one strategy with the resources of the other.

The most direct implication of the decision will be the allocation of resources between research and development. The research-intensive approach of the pioneer is more expensive, as of course it requires just as good development facilities as a development-intensive strategy. The company will inevitably be working much nearer to the boundaries of current knowledge, and this will mean that results are much less predictable. There will be a need for a certain amount of spare capacity in highly skilled and expensive scientists. These skilled people may very well form specialist cliques; they may value innovation much more highly than efficiency; some may be quite difficult to work with; their loyalty is as likely to be to their science as to the company—travelling hopefully may be more attractive to them than arriving.

All this suggests that the research-intensive strategy puts a fairly heavy burden on a company, in terms of costs and management skills. It is very dangerous to embark on it if the company is not able to carry it through. And this means being able to afford the right level of research investment, since half a research programme will achieve nothing; nor will a team of second-rate scientists. It also means adopting a productive management style. It is fairly clear that this will have to be a very open and unstructured style, allowing scope for individual responsibility, intuition and insight, without hierarchies and rigid time schedules. It has been shown[1] very clearly that in highly technical markets and those in which change is rapid—such as electronics—loose working structures are necessary to absorb the inevitably frequent changes of direction; a mechanistic approach simply cracks under the strain.

The improver, or development-intensive, strategy is the converse of this. What will be needed is relatively few scientists, but plenty of good development and production engineers and designers. They will have to be as interested in process development as in product development, and they will have to be backed by good technical and marketing intelligence; this will mean a fair investment in technical literature

[1] BURNS, T., and STALKER, G. M., *The management of innovation* (London, Tavistock Publications, 1961).

searches, attendance at conferences, participation in scientific societies and a good system of market reports on competitors' activities, both at home and abroad. The essence of the strategy is rapid response, and it suits a company whose style is one of getting things done.

The management problems for the project manager are rather less with a development-intensive strategy. Since much of the work is making relatively small improvements to something that exists, rather than inventing something which does not, it can be much more easily scheduled and planned in step-by-step processes. The R & D department tends to be nearer to production, and is very often originally briefed by market reports, and thus there are rather fewer problems of communication. On the other hand, being rather more rigid and needing to obtain quick results, it can be somewhat inflexible and vulnerable to managerial or administrative changes.

Effects on Market Choice

Once the technical innovation policy is settled, the project team can start to refine lists of possible markets and decide where, from a technological point of view, there might be opportunities.

The first action is simply to list the company's R & D assets and skills, analysing them as research-intensive or development-intensive. How many scientists has the company got? How many laboratory staff? What are they capable of doing? Are they free-ranging in ideas, or do they tend to dig more and more deeply into one technology? How many process engineers, production engineers, test engineers, designers, draughtsmen and so on? Again, what is their potential? What is the style of R & D management? What are the physical assets in R & D—buildings, laboratories, experimental equipment, pilot plant? How good is the current technical intelligence system? How much effort, if any, goes into technological forecasting?

While short-term change in R & D facilities is difficult, it is usually possible to add resources for the medium term. This could be through licensing arrangements or consultants, or through acquisition of a small company of research-heavy specialists. For small companies it is often a matter of using outside services such as the Patent Office library, government research stations, industrial research associations, universities and technical colleges; and there is a wide range of government grants towards research projects that could be exploited. The analysis of R & D assets must take such services into account.

Secondly, the question of new brand technical policy must be looked at from the point of view of the company's management style and personality. What sort of company does the management *want* to be— a high-risk, technical pioneer or a lower-risk, lower-reward, practical improver? Is the way the company is run at present better suited to an unstructured intuitive approach to problems or to orderly, step-by-step processes? Can the management cope, and does it really want to cope, with all the personal problems of a research-intensive operation? Could the company invest enough in research to be a pioneer? Is the management style sufficiently entrepreneurial to envisage raising money for high-risk research projects? And, in a fairly straightforward way, does the company personality make it a natural pioneer or a natural follower?

The project team then re-examines the list of possible markets that emerged from the first analysis of company assets. They could be broadly sorted into, say, three categories—technologically suitable; feasible, with some changes in R & D; unsuitable to this company. The sort of questions the project team will have to ask for each market are:

Is it a market with a much higher technical content than our current markets?

How near is the technology to our own?

Is there a history of rapid advances in technology?

Are there likely to be rapid changes in future? Are they more rapid than our R & D people are used to?

Is there already an established pioneer and an established improver? What sort of gap is there between them?

Are the main established companies in the market research-intensive or development-intensive?

Do they have access, through subsidiaries or associates, to basic research or development and design skills?

The questions are broad and the answers require fairly minimal knowledge of the markets and product types. One objective is to avoid costly and time-consuming investigations of technologies which might be ruled out on other grounds. If the project group knows too little to come to a firm conclusion about a market, then it is better to take the optimistic view, which might waste time later, than the pessimistic, which might lose a new brand opportunity.

MARKET DATA

It is only after going through these quite extensive analyses of company strengths and weaknesses and of its technological policy that it is worth looking at market data. This may seem a slightly surprising conclusion. It is in flat contradiction of the approach of many, maybe most, consumer goods companies. The norm is to start by looking for market opportunities and growth markets, or even listing the size of "all food markets" or "all leisure markets".

The most mindless of these activities is of course listing market sizes. Usually the only thing it achieves is to put off for several months difficult decisions of policy, while mounds of speculative and irrelevant figures are heaped up. But even the apparently more purposive searches for opportunities and growth markets are often based on myths.

The first myth is that there are such things as *natural market opportunities*, such that any intelligent person could identify them, provided he used the proper research techniques. There cannot be market opportunities in a vacuum. It would be very nice to have a car fuelled by water or a machine that not only washed and dried clothes, but also ironed them. But it would be ridiculous to call either of these a market opportunity at the moment; there is no hint of any company being able to exploit them. The market opportunity must be an opportunity for someone; and there is not much point in wasting time examining opportunities for companies other than one's own.

The second myth is that *growth markets* automatically provide the best opportunities. There is a dangerous half-truth here. Rapidly growing markets often do provide market opportunities, and declining markets usually do not. But there is nothing automatic about it. There are several reasons for this:

First, there is the error of looking for a market opportunity in a vacuum. There may well be a great opportunity in a rapidly growing market for one company, but not for another. The market for cars has been growing rapidly (if not smoothly) in the UK for many years and for some time will clearly continue to do so. It has been an excellent marketing opportunity for the big US car companies and for some of the UK car companies, when merged into large production units. It has not been a very great market opportunity for some of the smaller UK car companies, and it has been no sort of opportunity at all for ICI or Lever Brothers or Rowntrees. It is all a matter of who is capable of exploiting the market growth.

Secondly, there is a strong element of self-fulfilling prophecy about this. Just as a company can "prove" the product life-cycle theory by withdrawing support from a brand in temporary trouble, so the rate at which a market grows will depend very much on what manufacturers do to make it grow. Nobody, up to the 1960s, could have called the potato market in the UK a growth market. Potatoes have been for centuries a staple element of the diet; as a product they are solid, intransigent and unadventurous; expenditure on them as a percentage of all food spending tended to go down. Yet there have been two quite remarkable growth markets in potato products in the 1960s—instant mashed potato and potato crisps. Neither was very new. Smiths were making crisps in 1920, and instant mashed had had a bad name since Pom during the war. The crisp market was growing slowly in its sedate way, and instant mashed potato, despite reasonable success in the US, had been about as unsuccessful in the UK as cake mixes. Both were changed by companies *making* opportunities. Imperial Tobacco bought Golden Wonder, a small Scottish crisp company, and put some much-needed capital into it. Within five years it had become market leader and the market had more than doubled in size. In the instant mashed potato business, first Mars and then Cadbury *made* a growth market, partly by developing new products (thereby changing the rules of the game) and partly by determination to succeed. Some of the later entrants, such as Rank Hovis McDougall, came in when it actually was a growth market; but that was far from guaranteeing success for them.

Thirdly, sales growth is one element in profits, but it is not by any means the only one. Air travel has been one of the most rapidly growing markets since the war. But there are not many countries in which the airline business or aircraft manufacture does not have to be subsidized by the government. Some of the problems in exploiting a growth market *profitably* lie in the very fact that it is growing. It makes prediction harder, and it means that the company is constantly investing to meet tomorrow's needs—which is not only jam tomorrow for the shareholders, but also risky if the needs do not quite materialize. Many electronics-based businesses have run into this sort of trouble in their growth markets. So have consumer durables. Ownership of refrigerators in the UK has trebled over the last ten years, but in 1958 a 5·5 cu. ft refrigerator retailed at £75, in 1964 at £55 and in 1971 at about £45. There has not been a great deal of profit in it for manufacturers.

The UK frozen food industry is another example. It was quite clearly going to be a growth market, ever since Bird's Eye got it moving in the early 1950s. By 1960 it was vitally important for the smaller frozen food companies to forecast its future size reasonably accurately, in view of the very heavy investment needed in plant, storage and refrigerated distribution. Market statistics were quite reasonable and a great deal of US data was published. A straight-line projection, based on the average growth from 1956 to 1960, put the consumer market size for 1965 at £92 million, and a projection based on its accelerating growth rate put it at £104 million. A rather more sophisticated prediction, linking the pattern of US sales from 1949 with UK sales from 1958, resulted in a market size for 1965 of £146 million. Anyone in 1960 trying to make a forecast for 1965 had to

73

balance these rather widely differing figures with Bird's Eye's published forecast of £93 million sales for 1963. He also had to take into account the essential conservatism of the UK, slower development of self-service than in the US, smaller space in shops, lower ownership of refrigerators, and so on. Most forecasts were of a market worth at least £100 million in 1965. In fact, it came to only £74 million, according to Bird's Eye's published statements—substantially lower even than the straight-line projection. The effect of these over-estimates on investment and the subsequent low returns of some manufacturers are all too clear in retrospect.

The frozen food market, though undoubtedly a growth market, has not provided many opportunities for profit. Bird's Eye has done very well out of it, but it has been hard going for the other manufacturers. In fact, it has been some of the more opportunistic fringe companies that have done best—some of the companies supplying the manufacturers with goods and services, some of the companies offering restaurants a range of ready-cooked frozen meals, and so on. This

FIGURE 11. Success without a growth market

seems often the case with growth markets; it is not in the dead centre of the obvious growth area that the opportunities lie.

Rowntree's successful brand, After Eight thin mints, is a good contrast. The boxed chocolate market was not growing at all it when it was introduced; it had in fact declined in volume by as much as 15 per cent over the previous five years. Yet within four years this new brand—a good example of the blending of physical product and communications—was making a substantial contribution to the company's UK profits.

There is something very compulsive about the whole idea of natural growth markets, and the myth dies hard. Since people wondering about the future often come to the same sort of conclusions[1], there come to be fashions in predicting these growth markets. One of the fashions was once the aerosol, and some very extravagant predictions were made about the rate of growth. In fact the rate of growth was very fast. The Metal Box Company found it very profitable, and so for a time did the manufacturers of components. But many of the companies

FIGURE 12. More a brand than an aerosol

selling ranges of products in aerosol packs found their profits dwindling as sales went up. The price of the container was too great in relation to the value of the contents; manufacturers had little scope for building profits through product differentiation. Quickly competition and private label brands forced down prices. In the end, it has been the manufacturers with good *brands*—like Elida's Sunsilk hair

[1] e.g. BRECH, R., *Britain 1984: Unilever's forecast* (London, Darton, Longman and Todd, 1963); CALDER, N. (ed.), *The world in 1984* (London, Penguin Books, 1965); BRIGHT, J. R., "Opportunity and threat in technological change", *Harvard Business Review*, November–December 1963.

spray, launched in 1965—who succeeded; it was not much to do with the growth of aerosols *per se*.

There are many similar, seductive "natural growth markets" all the time. Levitt[1] writes of the illusory "leisure market", which in the abstract attracts so many manufacturers. It seems equally unlikely that some of the currently fashionable ones will provide good marketing opportunities for many companies—dish-washers, boats, mens' toiletries, electronics, slimming products, cassette TV, and so on.

Altogether, to start a development programme by searching for likely markets seems impractical and full of dangers; it is far more practical, sensible, realistic and progressive to look at market data only when the project team has throughly analysed the company's assets and their implications, its technological policy and very roughly where it reckons it might be going. Then it is a matter of collecting data on the relatively small number of markets that have emerged as feasible from this analysis.

Marketing men will be familiar enough with the main sources of information:

(i) Government statistics: Census of Distribution, Census of Production, National Income and Expenditure Blue Book, Trade and Navigation Reports, etc.

(ii) Government surveys: Family Expenditure Survey, National Food Survey, etc.

(iii) Media owners' and other published surveys: Nielsen data, IPC surveys of branded goods, Target Group Index, Economist Intelligence Unit, etc.

(iv) Manufacturers' associations: BEAMA, Brewers' Society, etc.

(v) Company reports;

(iv) Trade magazines and their editors; financial and business press;

(vii) Retailers and wholesalers, price lists, etc.

A great deal of this area is covered by Gordon Wills' excellent *Sources of Marketing Information*.[2] Perhaps the most valuable sources among the less used are the editors of trade magazines; they usually have a deep as well as a broad view of their industry, and since much of their day-to-day information comes from contacts with manufacturers, what they can say about an industry usually complements the available statistics ideally.

There will be great differences in the amount of data available on

[1] LEVITT, T., *The marketing mode*, p. 305 (New York, McGraw-Hill Book Company, 1969).

[2] WILLS, G., *Sources of marketing information* (London, Nelson, 1969).

different markets, but the sort of questions that the project team should endeavour to answer at this stage, for each market on the short list, are:

(i) What is the size of the market?

(ii) Is it growing, static or declining? Roughly how fast?

(iii) What sort of channels of distribution does it use? What are the special features of retailing in the market?

(iv) Who are the main manufacturers in the market? Roughly what shares do they have?

(v) What sort of companies are they? Big and diversified or small and specialized?

(vi) Are the companies vertically integrated? Does some of their success depend on involvement in both raw material and finished product?

(vii) Roughly how successful do they seem to be? Do they seem to be making a great deal of profit? Is there a rapid rate of disappearance of companies from the market?

(viii) Who are the consumers? How many and what sort of people?

(ix) What are the things about this market that make it most different from those we are already in?

(x) In what areas do the existing manufacturers seem most vulnerable?

This is all very rough and ready. But there is no great need, at this stage, to have a very detailed analysis of market data as they are now, when success is likely to depend on the company's ability to change the situation in the future. In the potato products' markets, a very detailed breakdown of market data would hardly have helped Cadbury and Imperial Tobacco to make their initial decisions to go into the market. Their very choice of market rapidly changed it all.

NEW BRAND POLICY: CHOICE OF MARKETS

The next stage, in formal terms, involves analysing all the data collected so far and relating it to the company's policies, in order to narrow down the areas of possible development to a manageable number. The result should be a very short list of markets, or submarkets, with a set order of priority; one of them is likely to be the market that the company is already in, or a new segment of it.

But this may be to look at it in too formal a way, and it is where the neat flow chart starts to be rather misleading. This is the stage at which the theory plus feedback approach and the teamwork really start. Up to this point it has been largely a matter of analysis and elimination of impossible markets. Now it is more a matter of positive choice—of making opportunities, not identifying them.

In fact, the project team has had one eye on the eventual choice of markets all along. The difference between this stage and the previous ones is that, while it has previously looked at markets with *optimism*, now it must look with *realism*. The object previously was to see in which markets the company *might* be able to introduce new brands (if it used all its skills to the full and maybe made a few improvements to them). At this point the aim is to work out in precisely which market it should start developing a new brand now.

The work involved is largely an extension of what has been done so far. In fact, the very discussion of the results of these stages by the project team will normally have cut down the list of possibles to a fairly small number. For instance, what may have seemed a natural development of a company distribution strength may be barely feasible technologically and turn out to be a very competitive market in which an old-established brand is very heavily entrenched; and thus be rejected, at any rate for the immediate future. It is here too that the top management should be involved in discussions. It may well be that other markets can be eliminated simply because the management does not want to go into them—even though they did not make this an element of new brand policy until the idea came up.

The remaining possibilities have to be put in rank order and cut down in number. Basically, what is needed is an *economic analysis* of each of the markets. So far, the project team has been considering whether the company could introduce new brands successfully into these markets at all, from the point of view of its production, R & D, marketing and financial skills and resources. Now what it must ask is whether the company might make profits out of doing so.

The economic analysis involves looking at a market or industry from a broad view; analysing what are the key factors affecting success, in terms of profits; predicting in what way, if any, they will change; examining the strengths and weaknesses of existing manufacturers, in relation to these key factors; finally rating the company's own potential in them.

It is partly a matter of going through the data already collected, but with financial implications in mind; partly of putting together more complete information on the market, its technology, its production and distribution systems, and so on. Published data may not be full enough, and it may be necessary to commission special surveys.

For instance, information would be collected, in the marketing area, on the products in the market, and hence the apparent need for a range of products. Would a new brand have to come in many varieties, or could it succeed as a single item? In the packaged cake market, for instance, where each brand has a long list of different varieties, it is hard to imagine success for a single line brand. What will the financial implications of this be? Clearly, heavy investment in a variety of plant—however small the geographical area to be covered. The need for a range of cakes is one of the key factors in the market from the point of view of economic analysis. So is the short shelf-life of cakes, which prevents stock-piling and governs distribution methods.

In the production area, plant location might be a key factor (as it is for brickmaking and cement production). Indeed, this may be more often a factor than is generally supposed. We tend often to believe that production skills are more mechanical than others, can be taught and learnt easily, and are therefore readily transferable to a new location. But there is a lot of evidence that local traditions of work and working methods change very slowly indeed. Making cars in the Liverpool or Glasgow areas is different from making cars in the Midlands; and there is a clear financial implication in the difference.

A particularly important question is the pricing method currently used in the market. Is it a "cost plus" price or is it determined by what the market will bear? If a market price, is it affected by excess capacity in the industry or by readily available substitutes from "another" market or by private label brands?

The precise areas to be considered will vary from market to market, but the questions to be answered are much the same. What is it that most distinguishes this market from others as far as profits are concerned? What are the absolute necessities, the key factors, for a company to make sustained profits in the market? How might these change or be changed? How do they relate to our products, production, technology and marketing?

Simply as a check list, here are some of the factors to be considered[1]:

Marketing

Product range: varieties and diversity, substitutes.

Marketing costs: advertising "entry fee", expenditure.

Distribution channels: minimum sales to sustain distribution, special transport, delivery/sales timing.

Length of product life, stability, cycles of demand.

Penetration of consumers, saturation of market.

Prices, pricing methods, margins, effects of price changes.

Basis of consumer's buying decision, brand loyalty.

---

[1] see PARKER, H., *Economic analysis of company strengths and weaknesses* (University of Bradford Management Centre, 1967).

Production
Plant: size, location, versatility, minimum economic size.
Machinery: type, size, price, versatility, rate of change.
Basic proportions of fixed and variable costs.
Effect of volume changes on production costs.
Raw materials: sources, price elasticity.

Technology
Processes used: variety, rate of change, relationship of process to product.
Lead time or development time for new products or processes.
Patents and other process obstructions.
Likelihood of technology change altering basic economics.
Effect of technology change: increased market or restructured market.

Industry structure
Number and type of companies in market, vertical or horizontal integration, local/national/international.
Industry production capacity.
Companies' access to finance, basic research, etc.
General level of profitability and return on investment.
Share prices: trends, cycles, p/e ratios.
Mergers, take-overs, entries and disappearances.
Trade associations and gentlemen's agreements.

At the end of this exercise the project team has a great deal of data on a few markets, some theories on what really matters most in each as far as profits are concerned, and ideas on whether their own company is the sort of company that could exploit these factors.

There is often an implication in the literature that the final choice of markets and their relative priority can be settled by some type of formula, based on return on investment. But the fact is that in any industry there can be wide variations in return on investment, and there is no reason why a new brand should automatically do better in a high-return industry than a low-return industry. It all depends on what the company is capable of doing and what is likely to happen in the industry (which are anyhow interrelated); and thus it will always be a matter of judgement. In fact, the final decision quite properly comes in the end to a question of what the company wants to do and in which area it feels that it might do things a little better than the companies already in the market.

If it all comes down to this sort of intuitive judgement, why go through all the analysis in the first place? It is really all a question of balance. If the choice had to be made between analysis and hunch, then history might well show hunch to be relatively more successful;

but there is no need for such a choice. What the analysis does is eliminate some absolute non-starters (which maybe hunch would have converted into expensive failures); ensure that a comprehensive list of possibilities is considered (many of which might otherwise have been missed); highlight the strengths of the company, so that they can be used, and the weaknesses, so that they can be corrected; and provide solid background data and a firm foundation for work on the markets that are finally chosen.

Two conferences on long-range planning[1], organized by the University of Bradford Management Centre, produced a number of papers describing how companies have approached problems of choice of new markets for development. P. J. Wright[2] described Massey-Ferguson's move into earth-moving equipment. By the early 1960s it looked as if the company's remarkable growth—through tractors, combine harvesters, diesel engines and light industrial equipment—would be hard to keep up. They analysed their strengths, in production, distribution and after-sales services. This led them, by the sort of processes described above, to earth-moving equipment. They then examined in detail the various segments of this market—crawler tractors, wheel loaders, hydraulic excavators, and so on. In addition to working out market sizes, the proportion of the market covered by each type of vehicle and so on, they discovered that the industry was structured so that each manufacturer tended to concentrate on one segment, producing a wide range of, say, crawler tractor models to cover all types of demand in that segment. Massey-Ferguson's economic analysis suggested to them that this was a matter of evolution rather than planning. Their idea for entering the market—no doubt, originally a matter of theory or intuition—was to provide an integrated range of products, using many of the same basic components, to cover the major parts of the three largest segments at the same time. They found that just nine products gave them a potential coverage of 87 per cent of earth-moving equipment volume sales. The interchangeability of components and small family of models not only cut down design and tooling costs for Massey-Ferguson; they also provided a more valuable franchise for their distributors. So a new brand of earth-moving equipment, based on a quite simple new idea, emerged from a systematic economic analysis and setting of strategy.

The Cadbury analysis of strengths[3] picked out its fairly broad

[1] "Long-range planning in British industry", 1967, and "Long-range planning for marketing and diversification", 1969.

[2] WRIGHT, P. J., *Expansion into an allied market* (University of Bradford Management Centre, 1969).

[3] HARVEY, J. C., *Strategies for diversification* (University of Bradford Management Centre, 1969).

81

experience of food technology; its experience in advertising, branding, packaging and presentation of consumer products; its skill in distribution; and, above all, the particular nature of the company personality. Cadbury's felt that their name denoted to people a standard of quality and quality control as much as a specialization in chocolate and cocoa products. (This was a bold belief and they were aware of the dangers in it; most manufacturers believe in the essential "quality" of their products, but very few have a *generalized* reputation for outstanding quality.) This analysis of their strengths led Cadbury, having made the obvious and not very committing decision to stick to food

FIGURE 13. **Results of a clear company strategy**

and drink, to look at markets where branding was not very developed and where a near-automatic reputation for quality would be of particular value. Marvel instant milk, Smash instant potato and the Cadbury range of packaged cakes were the result.

The Cadbury development was in many ways similar to Marks & Spencer's extension of their product range. Marks & Spencer's greatest strength has always been its buying. Clothing manufacturers were gradually induced by M & S to adopt standards of specification and quality control that they had never known before, often to their own

82

very great advantage. What M & S saw was that this special strength could be applied in other areas; and this was the start of their very successful entry into private label food retailing. As with Cadbury, it was in areas where food was poorly branded and of variable quality that they had particular success. For instance, they revolutionized the cake business, and still account for about 10 per cent of all cake sold.

Of course, the most frequent result of working out a new brand strategy is to put as first priority existing markets or new segments of them—often eventually inventing new segments. For all their success in instant milk, cakes and instant potato, Cadbury have much more frequently introduced new chocolate confectionery brands. However, in the end most companies have to develop new brands outside the most familiar markets, and this is where the principle of interlocking chains is best used, each new area being based on an existing strength. Batchelors Foods Limited, which was Batchelors Peas Limited when Unilever bought it in 1943, was almost wholly dependent on one product and one process in the middle 1950s[1]—canned peas. The development into Surprise quick-dried peas was clearly based on the company's knowledge and skills in the buying of peas, plus the development of better dehydration techniques. It was a relatively small step from this process development to dried packet soups, though it was certainly helped by borrowing experience from US associates. And ultimately to Vesta dried meals. It is interesting that some of the company's unsuccessful new brands do not appear to have such direct links with points of strength. Their steak and kidney pie, for instance, never did very well, while the Fray Bentos brand, which was firmly based on its company's strengths in meat, has dominated the market.

There is of course no guarantee of success if a company uses this sort of sensible step-by-step planning to reach a new brand strategy; and no guarantee of failure if it does not. The Rank Organization, for instance, has for many years been developing new services from the base of its film interests. By examining its skills and using the same approach as "Marketing Myopia" the company decided that it was in the entertainment business. Most of the new services, such as bowling alleys, have had a logical connection with the entertainment business or with the equipment used in the film business, but none has been out-standingly successful. What has worked dramatically well for Ranks has been its connection with and development of Xerox, and the crucial decision to go into the equipment-renting business; neither of which has any very close connection with the film industry.

The only sensible approach is to use both analytical planning and

[1] GOODALL, A. J., *Long-range planning in practice* (University of Bradford Management Centre, 1967).

intuitive ideas. From this point onwards, personal and creative skills have a far more important part to play than the strictly analytical.

CONSUMERS AND CONSUMPTION

The project team has now, after discussion with management, settled on a very small number of markets in which to try to develop a major new brand. But of course this begs the question of what is meant by "market".[1] The word can be used in a very broad sense, such as "the packaged foods market", or in a very narrow sense, such as "the premium-price air-dried polythene-wrapped root vegetable flake market". The first is so broad that nothing very specific follows from entry into it; the second is so narrow that (if it could exist at all) it would be impossibly restricting to decide to enter it. The argument so far has assumed a sensible middle course, referring to medium-sized chunks, such as the earth-moving equipment market or the instant potato market or the crisp market or the upholstered furniture market.

In any case, now is the point at which the decisions must be translated into the sort of consumer language suggested by "Marketing Myopia". So far, the project team has been looking from the company outwards. Now they must start the other end and look at the final demand and what it might be in the future, at consumers and their pattern of needs, wants and desires, and at their use of substitutes, which may not tie up at all well with the inevitable neatness of marketing men's definitions. They must think more of going into the breakfast business than into the ready-to-eat compressed wheat flake biscuit cereal business.

The starting point is consumers' current behaviour and current attitudes. Research is used to discover who buys, when, where and how; who uses, when, where and how; who thinks what about which brands already in the market and about which substitute for them. This provides background data from which the project team works out where there might be opportunities for a new brand.

It is from this stage onwards that the theory of the successful new brand helps particularly. It not only provides a constant sense of direction; it also ensures that the consumer research is done with a purpose, that its results will be usable, comprehensive and realistic—without wasting large sums on assembling masses of "interesting" data that gathers dust on the bookshelf. To collect all the consumer research listed below would of course be expensive and time-consuming, and no single market is likely to need it all. But in general it is

[1] Sissors, J. Z., "What is a market?" *Journal of Marketing*, July 1966.

surprising how cheap this basic research is, compared with the other costs of new brand development, as long as the project team knows what sort of answers it is looking for.

1. Buying and Using Research

(A) BUYING

Retail audits can give useful basic data about the split of sales into product types, brands, sizes, prices; by shop sizes and types. It is expensive research for these immediate purposes, as it reveals relatively little about consumers' buying habits. However, since the marketing men are almost bound to want it at the pilot marketing stage and since they will find it hard to use then without back data, it can be worth buying even at this early stage. This sort of information is, of course, less easily available and less useful, as one moves from cheap mass-market consumer goods towards durables and industrial goods.

Consumer panel data are particularly valuable, since they aggregate the buying patterns of individual households, to show frequencies of buying, duplication of purchase of different brands, differential buying habits by segments, and so on. In addition, they are the best means of monitoring prices paid, special offers taken up, and so on. Again, panel research is economic only for reasonably frequently bought consumer goods.

Ad hoc consumer surveys of a fairly straightforward kind can ask questions about who buys, when, where and how. This can usually be covered at the same time as questions about usership.

Observation is a research method which is used all too infrequently. Quite a small-scale operation, with people stationed in shops to note the behaviour of buyers of the product category, can often raise important hypotheses for checking by the more quantified methods.

(B) BUYING DECISIONS

It is surprising that, in spite of its very obvious importance, relatively little research has been done in most markets into the actual buying decision. It is quite clear that most people do not always buy all or exclusively the things they entered a shop to buy. It is also clear that there are usually influences on the buyer from the rest of the family or other users.

System Three[1] have done a good deal of work here on consumer goods. While their view is that each market has its own particular system, they have been able to categorize six sorts of buying decision:

[1] SMITH, V. A., *Exploring the buying decision* (System Three (communication No. 8), September 1970).

(i) Automatic routine (e.g. tea; washing powders; weekday cigarettes)
(ii) Unguided but regular (e.g. canned fruit; hardware)
(iii) Anxious occasional (e.g. gifts; large toys; gourmet foods)
(iv) High cost/long deliberation (e.g. cars; furniture; holidays)
(v) Intensely personal (e.g. clothes; records; weekend cigarettes)
(vi) Impulse (books; records; clothes)

The research techniques used by System Three, nearly always in combination, have been intensive interviews, group discussions, confrontations of buyers and non-buyers, observation of buying in shops, followed by intensive interviews and re-enactment of the decision, and spot checks in stores. The most valuable method has been observation of the way buyers approach the product type, how they examine brands, how they handle them, whether they read the pack and so on. Final assessments of buying decisions take into account how automatic they appear to be; how uncertain the buyer is about the product's suitability; level of interest and involvement in the product; the role of accident and impetus; the influence of deliberation before buying and who does the deliberating; the nature and strength of imagined post-purchase satisfaction.

The buying decision in industrial goods tends to be even more complex, and it would be very rash to try to enter a new industrial market without some idea of which people make most contribution to what sort of decisions, and the criteria—both rational and emotional—by which they do it. This must inevitably be a matter of intensive interviews with samples of all the types of people—management, department heads, engineers, users, buyers—who can affect the decision. One recent study[1] examined the buying decisions involved in the electronics, engineering and chemical industries; and published details of nine individual decisions (laser, effluent plant, multi-point temperature indicator, climatic cabinet, small computer, granulator, very low frequency tracking receiver, micro densitometer and spectral analyser). In most cases the decision-making process started at the operational or laboratory-bench level. Department heads tended to formalize the need for new equipment that had been pointed out at the operational level. Nearly always several "technical" people were involved and the final approval for the expenditure came from above—general management or the Board, who might be relatively ignorant of the detailed needs and specifications. There was a certain conflict between the management's and the engineers' opinions about the

[1] SHANKLEMAN, E., *A study of industrial buying decisions* (New Science Publications, 1970).

importance of the role played by the other. Quite clearly, this is an area where research provides essential information.

(C) USING

Fairly standard *survey* and *observation* methods are used to establish who uses the product type and who uses different brands, when, where and how; how users and buyers overlap or differ; the relationship between primary and secondary users; different people using brands for different purposes or the same people using brands in different ways on different occasions; duplication of usership of different brands; and so on. Normally intensive interviews would be used to set up preliminary hypotheses, to be followed up by quantitative or semi-quantitative research.

In markets where there is likely to be a complex pattern of use, diary studies can often supplement people's memories.[1] For instance, in the breakfast cereal market where different members of a family will typically eat several different brands during quite short periods, a diary of who ate how many platefuls of which at what meal is almost essential, to establish patterns of consumption with any accuracy.

There are two approaches which are somewhat unusual in consumer research, but particularly important to this stage of new brand development. They are unusual only because research companies are usually too narrowly briefed, not because the research is particularly difficult or expensive.

The first involves working out what are the substitutes for the brands in the formally defined market. In one sense, a very large range of products is in competition with each single type, since all are competing for the limited amount of money available for spending. Even in a more meaningful sense, there are many different food products competing with, say, breakfast cereals—ranging from porridge to cups of coffee, via fruit, eggs, toast, milk, pills, biscuits and anything else which satisfies people's needs at "breakfast time". Surveys can get some hints of these substitutes directly, by asking people what else they eat at breakfast, what they would do if they had run out of breakfast cereals, and so on; and they can discover on what sort of situations each would act as a substitute. A more elaborate method can ask consumers to judge the extent to which products are similar or dissimilar to each other. This might be valuable for, say, packaged desserts, where there is a huge number of products which are different in form—like jelly and suet pudding—and which may or may not be substitutes for

---

[1] BATES, B. A., and BERMINGHAM, J., *Short-term diaries: Their use in collecting detailed consumption data* (ESOMAR conference, 1968).

each other. Again, diary studies can be especially valuable, in that they are nearer to measuring what people actually do rather than what they think they do.

The point of doing this substitute research is that it shows people's behaviour in consumer-defined markets, not producer-defined markets. And in an indirect way it can show the weaknesses of the traditional product field; for instance, perhaps the desire for something solid and warming at breakfast time or the need for visual excitement and variety in desserts.

The second approach also stems from looking at the use of products from the point of view of the user. Most brands are consumed as part of a system or sequence of events; they have a role to play in the system, and it is hardly possible to evaluate the role without knowing about the system as a whole. It is hard to know what is the complete range of satisfactions given by a dessert if one does not know at which meals it is eaten, who is eating it, with whom, when, for how long, what each eats and drinks before, after or while eating the dessert. It is surprising how often we are ignorant about the simple mechanics of these systems. Again, it is partly a matter of a standard question and answer survey, partly a matter of observation studies.

2. Attitude Research

The sort of attitude research needed goes back to the anatomy of the successful new brand. The new brand must be relevant to the whole range of people's needs, wants or desires—not just the functional needs. It must be a coherent totality—not a collection of bits. It must be a unique blend of appeals to the senses, the reason and the emotions.

Thus what consumer attitude research has to do here is to examine the whole range of needs and desires, to make a map of people's current attitudes to the different brands or substitutes at the sensual, rational and emotional levels; and also at the level of totalities, the personalities of brands.

(A) LANGUAGE

Any structured consumer research must ask people to respond to specific ideas, specifically stated. There are no great problems of language in dealing with the use of brands, but there are with attitude research. It must clearly avoid committing people to agreeing or disagreeing with a view or a brand attribute expressed in language that is strange to them. This is bound to happen to some extent, if a standard questionnaire is used, but at least surveys should use the highest common factor of consumer language.

Thus the starting point of attitude research in a new market is to establish as far as possible the language and imagery that people use. Normally group discussions are the best source of information, since the interaction of members of the group brings people's natural language out—they are not giving considered answers to questions. But intensive open-ended single interviews can be valuable too. A more formal method used has been the repertory grid technique, borrowed from clinical psychology and G. A. Kelly's personal construct theory.[1] The basic form of repertory grid research involves presenting the respondent with three cards, selected randomly from a pack, each of which carries the name of one of the brands in the market; he is then asked to say in what way two of the three are similar to each other—and different from the third. He then sorts the remaining cards into two groups, according to whether they conform in this dimension to the pair or the odd brand. The whole process is then repeated until the respondent runs out of attributes on which he thinks brands differ. There are certainly many doubts as to whether these dimensions do in fact combine to produce a total view of a brand. But this process is reasonably claimed to produce an exhaustive list of consumer-derived dimensions and they should be meaningful to at least some consumers.

(B) SENSUAL RESPONSES

Blind product tests are traditionally used to establish people's attitudes to brands at the sensual level. It is clearly necessary to discover how the physical products in the market compare with each other, separately from their names, packs and reputations, in terms of their looks, weight, smell, taste, texture, shape and so on. There are two particular problems here, both deriving from most people's very insensitive sensual discrimination.

First, it is often necessary to use extended product tests, since repeated use of two products may very well alter perceptions of the relationship between them. This is particularly true of food products or cigarettes, where the first taste may well give a very different impression from a week's use.

Secondly, it is often worth running parallel tests of products in their standard market-place packs. Undoubtedly taste and performance are modified by people's expectations. Comparison of blind and named tests can very valuably hint which of the differences perceived are "in the product" and which "in the mind".

All this makes product testing an expensive business. But it seems

[1] FROST, W. A. K., and BRAINE, R. L., "The application of the repertory grid technique to problems in market research", *Commentary* (now *Journal of the Market Research Society*), July 1967.

very fundamental to developing a new brand. Laboratory analysis of competitive brands must be done too, but it is hardly enough to give a clear impression of consumers' likes and dislikes.

This research should end with establishing a language for product attributes, identifying a number of physical scales (like soft/hard, sweet/savoury, heavy/light) which are important to the product type, and a clear idea of where current brands are positioned in relation to each other on each scale.

(C) RATIONAL RESPONSES

In much the same way, a series of scales is drawn up, which express formal beliefs about the product type—people's rational responses about what the brands contain, what they do, their function and purpose, their suitability for certain needs and groups of people, and so on. The choice of scales will derive from the qualitative research done originally to bring out consumers' language—for instance, from simple analysis of the frequency of mention and order of mention of attributes. Although many elaborate and mechanistic systems have been advocated, selecting these scales and deciding which are the fundamental ones, both now and in the future, must ultimately be a matter of judgement. So it is usually better at this stage not to be too ruthless in weeding out the less likely ones.

Then structured attitude research is used to place the individual brands on each scale. Semantic differentials are often used, but there is some evidence[1] that, despite appearances, greater sensitivity can be got from a simpler approach. This presents people with a list of brands and asks them to name as many or as few as they like, in relation to each end of the scale separately. (Which of these brands would be sweet? Which would be savoury?) One of the advantages of the simpler approach is that it can more easily be reproduced; it is clearly very valuable to repeat the exercise when the new brand is on the market.

In addition to this map of formal beliefs about brands, it is worth having the results of more open-ended questions relating the brands to their substitutes and to the system in which they have a role.

(D) EMOTIONAL RESPONSES

Perhaps the most crucial area for research and the one that will most stimulate ideas from the project team is that of people's feelings about brands, the real satisfactions they offer and the roles that they play. This is where the research must be particularly unstructured, and allow

[1] JOYCE, T., "Techniques of brand image measurement", *Market Research Society conference*, 1963.

90

people to talk freely in their own language and with their own imagery. It inevitably depends for its success on the skills of the researcher in stimulating people's responses and interpreting them—not only what they say, but the way they say it, their expressions and gestures.

This research must be wide in coverage, and it must certainly inquire into the whole consumption system. We cannot easily make progress in inventing new brands until we get some idea of the real motives that lie behind the system. Why, for instance, do people want to wash clothes? What is the balance between their different desires—a crisp feel, avoidance of disease, prestige, expression of personality, and so on? What is the real significance of whiteness? Why are some clothes washed more than others? It is fairly clear that the simple-minded answer "to get them clean" only scratches the surface.

Again, though emotional values are often much harder to identify or to name, there tends to be a small number of fundamental scales in each market; and the object of the research is to identify them and see how brands are related to each other on them. For instance, in breakfast cereals the most important may be traditional/good for you $v.$ fun/self-indulgence; in cakes, home-made-ish $v.$ factory-made; in paint, for people who like the effect $v.$ for people who like the painting itself; in washing powders, mild/good natured $v.$ efficient/brisk; in garden products, for the casual/sporadic gardener $v.$ for the careful/obsessive gardener.

(E) BRAND PERSONALITY

Even harder is research that maps out the positions of brands as a whole, as coherent totalities—which is what people buy. A whole range of projective techniques has been borrowed from clinical psychology and used with rather little success. The most successful methods seem to be the simplest; that is, asking respondents to imagine brands as people, or to imagine the personality of the people who make or sell or use the different brands. Provided that the research situation has been set up sympathetically, the simple question "If Brand A came to life, what sort of person would it be?" can stimulate a rich flow of extremely perceptive comment. People are much more used to talking about other people than about things. Much of the research about the attributes of brands is asking people to express views about things in a way that is foreign to them—starting at the pieces and working towards the whole. Brand personality research works because it starts with the whole, and encourages people to go on from there to the pieces.

3. Market Segmentation

The theory of market segmentation[1] is a very attractive one for identifying opportunities in new brand development, and it has been widely advocated. This is the theory that the market for any product type is made up of sub-groups or segments of consumers, each of which has slightly different needs, wants or desires; thus the task of the new brand developer is to identify the sub-groups, discover which of them is being least well satisfied by current brands and design a new brand specifically for that sub-group. It all seems very logical. The trouble is that it does not seem to work very well in practice.[2]

The problems have mostly lain in the difficulty of identifying homogeneous sub-groups with a special purchasing behaviour. Most of the early market segmentation approaches, which used demographic breakdowns, fairly predictably failed; and it was thought that this was because the categories were too crude. But it was found that sociographic and personality variables did very little better. One US survey[3] used seventeen different demographic, sociographic and personality variables, to sort people into homogeneous groups, but they were apparently able to account for only four per cent of the variance in consumer behaviour. In the UK, the elaborate Londoner survey,[4] which segmented people by fundamental personality characteristics, was embarrassingly inept at explaining brand choice.

The situation is perhaps summed up best by the data produced by the Target Group Index, which is the largest comprehensive survey of usage of consumer goods in the UK. This shows that in most product fields there are undoubtedly differences between the users of different brands, in their social class and age composition, their ownership of goods, their media habits and attitudes to life; but the differences are

[1] e.g. AGOSTINI, J. M., A method of market segmentation, ESOMAR congress, 1965; JOYCE, T., and CHANNON, M. R., "Classifying market survey respondents", *Journal of the Royal Statistical Society*, Vol. 15, No. 3, 1966; SMITH, W., "Product differentiation and market segmentation as alternative marketing strategies", *Journal of Marketing*, July 1956; WELLS, W. D., TIGERT, D. J., "Activities, interests and opinions", *Journal of Advertising Research*, August 1971; YANKELOVICH, D., "New criteria for market segmentation", *Harvard Business Review*, March–April 1964.

[2] BARNETT, N. L., "Beyond market segmentation", *Harvard Business Review*, January–February 1969; COLLINS, M., "Market segmentation—the realities of buyer behaviour", *Journal of the Market Research Society*, July 1971; KASSARJIAN, H. H., "Personality and consumer behaviour: a review", *Journal of Marketing Research*, November 1971.

[3] FRANK, R. E., *Market segmentation research: Findings and implications* (Graduate School of Industrial Administration, Purdue University, 1966); FRIEND, I., and KRAVIS, I. B., "New light on the consumer market", *Harvard Business Review*, January–February 1957.

[4] *Londoner Survey* (London, Associated Rediffusion Limited, 1962).

almost invariably much less striking than their similarities. That is, there are tendencies to consumer segmentation, but there is normally no question of there being groups so clearly distinguished by needs or desires that they will use Brand A but not Brand B. There are of course a few clear cases of segmentation, but they are usually based on rather obvious functional differences—razor blades, lipstick, tricycles, rosary beads—and refer to product types rather than brands. Apart from these, it seems that in the UK social class differences, and all that goes with them, are still the main discriminators.

It is not altogether surprising that this sort of market segmentation does not work very well. Analysis of consumer panel data[1] shows that in many markets the duplication of use of any two brands is highly predictable, and is simply a function of the level of use of each. This sort of predictability makes it unlikely that there is very much clear-cut segmentation of consumers of the conventional type—the "always use Brands L and M, never use Brands P and Q" type. Other studies[2] show that in most markets most people have a repertoire of acceptable brands, which they tend to buy in cycles of different frequencies. And there is much evidence that in many markets there is a positive need for variety.[3] The idea of there being one set of Brand A users and another set of Brand B users is clearly very simplistic.

A development of market segmentation theory is product segmentation, which seems more promising. The idea here is that people differentiate among brands in a market according to their perceptions of the brands' attributes; and on any buying occasion they are more likely to choose a brand whose personality and characteristics they prefer.[4] The only measurable factor that distinguishes the people who buy Brand A from those who do not (or those for whom Brand A makes up a high proportion of purchases from those for whom it makes up a low proportion) is their liking for Brand A. Though some of the same objections apply to product segmentation as to consumer segmentation, it is at least consistent with the findings[5] that

[1] EHRENBERG, A. S. C., and GOODHARDT, G. J., "A model of multi-brand buying", *Journal of Marketing Research*, February 1970.

[2] McDONALD, C. D. P., "What is the short-term effect of advertising?", ESOMAR congress 1970 and *Admap*, November 1970.

[3] REYNOLDS, W. H., "More sense about market segmentation", *Harvard Business Review*, September–October 1965.

[4] BARNETT, N. L., "Beyond market segmentation", *Harvard Business Review*, January–February 1969; KUEHN, A. A., and DAY, R. L., "Strategy of product quality", *Harvard Business Review*, November–December 1962; ZIFF, R., "Psychographics for market segmentation", *Journal of Advertising Research*, April 1971.

[5] EHRENBERG, A. S. C., "Towards an integrated theory of consumer behaviour", *Journal of the Market Research Society*, October 1969, pp. 307–13.

the difference between purchases of brands in the short run lies in the number of people buying, rather than the amounts bought. The successful brand simply has a *higher* regular penetration than the unsuccessful brand, not necessarily a *different* type of penetration. The significant difference in implications between this theory and consumer segmentation theory is that the new brand must aim to have a unique blend of characteristics, not look for a unique group of consumers.

In fact, the conclusions one must reach from any study of market segmentation are:

(i) At best, it is a matter of tendencies.

(ii) The best way of working out these tendencies is by examining attitudes to brands in the ways described above, since the segmentation is by perceived brand characteristics.[1] More elaborate techniques, such as the Automatic Interaction Detector programme,[2] can quantify the tendencies, using attitude data; but it does not seem particularly helpful to have such tendencies quantified.

(iii) The basic principle is that the *brand sets its own pattern*. The brand, as it were, chooses its consumers, not vice versa. The right target group cannot be finally selected until the brand has been invented. This apparent circularity (the right market segment for a new brand is the people who are attracted to it) has important implications for the selection of groups of consumers for research at later stages.

4. Analysis of Opportunities

If these are the conclusions, then it is tempting to think that there may be techniques for revealing the opportunities for new brands, by systematically examining people's perceptions of the characteristics of existing brands. That is, by looking for gaps along scales of attributes which are not yet filled by a brand.

A number of elaborate systems of "gap analysis" were set up, and were fairly enthusiastically received, a few years ago. The most carefully worked out system[3] aimed to produce an exhaustive list of such gaps, using a special computer program to do so. First the repertory

[1] SKELLY, F. R., and NELSON, E. H., "Market segmentation and new product development" (Market Research Society conference, 1966); O'MULLOY, J. B., "Research and the development of new products", *Admap*, August 1969.

[2] ASSAEL, H., "Segmenting markets by group purchasing behaviour: An application of the AID technique", *Journal of Marketing Research*, May 1970.

[3] CLEMENS, J., and THORNTON, C., "Evaluating non-existent products", *Admap*, May 1968; MORGAN, N., and PURNELL, J., "Isolating openings for new products in a multi-dimensional space", *Journal of the Market Research Society*, July 1969; STEFFLRE, V., "Concept and product development and testing: A

grid technique was used to generate a complete list of bi-polar attitude dimensions; these were then edited and transformed into seven-point semantic differential scales. Next each of the brands in the market (and often substitutes too) was rated on each of the scales. These figures were the basic input data for the gap analysis computer program. What the computer program did was simulate multi-dimensional space and then identify gaps on, say, fifteen dimensions simultaneously; it would then print out where the gaps were, in order of size of gap. As a very simple example, using just two dimensions, gap analysis might show for shampoos that there were brands in

the gentle/cosmetic quarter (Sunsilk, Breck, etc.)
the strong/medicated quarter (Vosene, Loxene, etc.)
and   the gentle/medicated quarter (Clinic);
but not the strong/cosmetic quarter.

The gap would therefore be for a strong cosmetic type of shampoo. This example is not as unfair as it sounds; inevitably most of the gaps exist because nobody would want a brand with that particular combination of characteristics.

Gap analysis: Shampoos

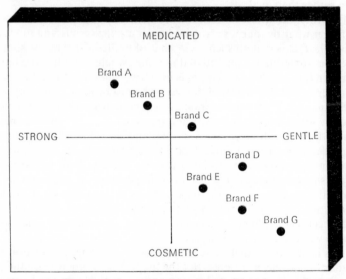

FIGURE 14. Hypothetical example shows the principles of gap analysis (on two dimensions only)

soup to nuts approach" (ESOMAR seminar, November 1970); THORNTON, C., "Ranking new product openings in multi-dimensional space" (Market Research Society conference, 1970).

The theory of gap analysis has been well argued and sounds very logical. As Pollitt[1] points out, "It is only when you try to track down the significant products it has led to, or attempt to grapple with the problems of applying it yourself, that the problems crop up." But the theory of the successful new brand does suggest flaws in the argument. And consideration of the purposes of the exercise does suggest that, however tempting, this sort of gap analysis could easily waste time and money.

First, the input data come entirely from considered responses to questions about how brands differ. Yet the successful new brand works by having a blend of appeals at the sensual and emotional levels, as well as the rational. Gap analysis is inevitably one-sided.

Secondly, it assumes that brands are made up, as it were, by adding together a finite set of attributes. But it is the totality of the brand and the effect that this has had on the interrelationship of attributes that matter. Gap analysis seems to be starting from the wrong end.

Thirdly, any sort of analysis of current attitudes to brands is itself historical. It cannot show to what extent a dynamic new factor could change the rules. The future does not follow logically and deductively from the past. Gaps and opportunities will emerge through imagination rather than analysis.

Fourthly, the whole mathematical expression of gap analysis tends to forget what the purpose is; who has to use the results and in what way. The fact is that all such research is of limited value unless someone does something at the end of it that they would not otherwise have done. In this case, the something is inventing a new brand that works. In other words, the results of the research must be more than simply a valid analysis. They must operate as a *language* between the consumer and the inventors of the new brand (research men, production men, marketing men, designers and so on); and they must *stimulate* new hypotheses and new totalities. Gap analysis runs into the same sort of problem as those heavyweight attitude surveys that purport to establish mathematically the relative importance of attributes in a market, and that print out the results as the number of standard deviations between the mean of the brands and the "ideal" brand (whatever that might be): after a great deal of time and money, nobody knows what to do with the figures.

This is not to say that there is no value in studying the position of brands on various attributes. But the more stimulating way is almost certainly the "naïve" way[2]; looking at them individually, and specu-

[1] POLLITT, S., "A practical approach to new products and new concepts", *Admap*, March 1970, p. 87.
[2] GREENHALGH, C., "Generating new product ideas", ESOMAR congress 1971 and *Admap*, September, October and November 1971.

lating what the gaps mean and why they are there and whether they could profitably be filled.

In any case, the real purpose of collecting all the information on consumers and consumption is not to reveal opportunities *directly*. It is to provide reliable background data as a starting-point for working out ideas and inventing new brands. The invention itself is by the theory-experiment-feedback method, and as often as not starts with introspection (that is, personal knowledge) rather than research knowledge.

How the ideas for new brands are generated is dealt with on page 100. But the main constriction on ideas is what it is technically possible to make. Equally, it is technological change most of all that changes the rules of the market. So before starting to invent the new brand idea, it is necessary to get some knowledge of what technological changes are likely to be feasible. This is of course particularly important in industrial markets.

TECHNOLOGY

There are two approaches to getting an idea of the limitations and opportunities set by technology. The first is technological forecasting, which is essential for any company with a pioneer technical strategy. The second is monitoring competitors' activities and, if possible, anticipating their plans; this is particularly important to the company with an improver strategy.

1. *Technological forecasting* is still undoubtedly more of an art than a science, just as sales forecasting is, and it can be slightly alarming when two eminent forecasters reach different conclusions. But the object is not so much to predict precisely what form new technology will take or precisely when the next "breakthrough" will come, as to assess the probability of future developments and their effects on the market and the company. Part of the value of doing it lies in the very processes of thought and the stimulus to technical people.

In fact, although technological forecasting may seem much more mysterious than sales forecasting and has a very formidable literature,[1] there is no particular reason why it should be much more difficult or inaccurate. This is because new technologies do not normally arrive suddenly out of the blue. They are usually the practical application of physical phenomena or physical relationships which have been well known for some time. Even when there are fundamental process changes, which appear to happen overnight, they are usually the result

[1] There is a comprehensive bibliography in JANTSCH, E., *Technological forecasting in perspective* (OECD, Paris, 1967).

of a whole series of small and apparently insignificant performance changes.

In many ways, technological forecasting is more dependent on knowledge, while sales forecasting is more dependent on interpretation and understanding relationships—which may be harder. But both depend, as J. B. Quinn's excellent review[1] puts it, "on careful analyses of past experience, combined with the insights of competent and imaginative people". It is unfortunate that the whole area of technological forecasting has developed a quite horrific and wholly unnecessary battery of mystical jargon words.

Quinn lists five basic approaches to technological forecasting:

(A) DEMAND ANALYSIS

One theory is that clearly perceived demand is the primary force stimulating technical change, and that if the demand is strong enough it will call forth the human resources necessary to solve the technical problems. Some of the most dramatic and quickest advances have been made in wartime, when there is an overwhelming and narrowly defined public demand. This can apply to prestige war too; demand in the US to "get a man on the moon" clearly led to advances in space flight technologies. One could speculate that public demand could lead today to improvements in car safety, air pollution control, noise control and waste disposal methods; but it is certainly judgemental—demand has not, for instance, notably led to improvements in house-building technology.

The trouble is that forecasting demand is itself very speculative, and at best it can give no hint of the sort of technology that will emerge. For instance, it could be predicted that in the 1980s there will be a shortage of natural leather, and thus there will be an overwhelming demand for some substitute. However, as DuPont has discovered, it is far from clear when this will happen, how strong the new demand will be, for precisely what and what sort of technology will be required.

(B) THEORETICAL LIMITS TEST

This involves pushing a known apparatus or phenomenon to its theoretical limits and then trying to visualize the implications; that is, the new uses to which it might be put and the effect they might have on other technologies. While it tends to lead to science fiction results, that is better than developing no new ideas at all.

(C) PARAMETER ANALYSIS

This approach is central to most forecasting systems. It is a matter of

[1] QUINN, J. B., "Technological forecasting", *Harvard Business Review*, March–April 1967.

selecting performance characteristics; plotting the predicted rate of their advance, often by extrapolating historical trends (Wills[1] gives a good example of this in plotting advances in lumens per watt in lamps); documenting the assumptions used in predicting ranges of values; estimating the likelihood of reaching the projection at the forecast time. A combination of this sort of parameter analysis and the

Development of lumens per watt

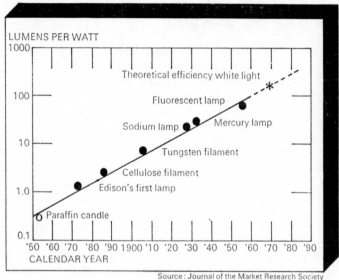

Source: Journal of the Market Research Society

FIGURE 15. **Forecasting technological change by extrapolating historical trends (Wills)**

theoretical limits test can give some sort of hint as to when advances can only come through switching over to an entirely new technology. For instance, it could help forecast under what conditions plastics might replace steel in building or car manufacture.

(D) SYSTEMS ANALYSES

Analyses of complete technical systems can help to pinpoint the weak links in the chain, thereby identifying opportunities—improvement in the weak link would very often either put up performance in the whole system or cut down costs in the other links. Another systems analysis approach sets hypothetical future problems and works out what technologies would be needed to solve them. Impact studies start

[1] WILLS, G., "Technological forecasting: The art and its management", *Journal of the Market Research Society*, April 1968.

with the question "If a new technology could achieve these capacities, what would the results be?"

(E) SCIENTIFIC SURVEYS
These involve reviewing the work done in relevant scientific disciplines, to see how much progress is being made and how relevant it might be to the company's technology. For the pioneer company it is a matter of supplementing the company's own basic research by bringing it in contact with relevant academic work in other areas, and by formally trying to predict where it will lead.

2. *Monitoring competitors' activities* is in much the same way largely a matter of using common sense and imagination. The techniques are valuable partly as disciplines, to make sure that people do actually sit down and try to monitor competitors' activities; partly as stimuli to setting about the job in an imaginative way.

Quinn lists three approaches:

(A) Analysing the product life cycle in a market in the past can give a fairly good idea of when competitors are likely to be introducing technological changes.

(B) Technological mapping is a method of evaluating competitors' strengths. From publications, patents and commercial intelligence sources the competitors' status in each technological activity judged relevant can be mapped out. Over time, changes in the "map" can indicate where the competitors are developing their potential.

(C) Strategic analyses, much like those used for working out one's own policy, can suggest where competitors will place their technological emphasis. This is particularly valuable when working out the implications of a takeover or the setting up of a new laboratory.

In addition, there are the fairly standard procedures of attending conferences, monitoring competitors' literature and patent applications, analysing their products, examining trade media and scientific abstracts, looking overseas.

Both technological forecasting and predicting competitors' actions are full of uncertainties; but they can be very rewarding. The rewards will come not only in the forecasts themselves, but also in the technological insights, ideas and stimulus that come from considering the future in a systematic way. They can bring the project team well on the way to working out specific new brand concepts.

IDEAS

It is often assumed that getting ideas is one of the hardest parts of the whole new brand development process. There are many conferences and articles about it,[1] and certainly many companies make rather heavy weather of it. In fact, having new brand ideas is one of the easiest parts. (Getting them to work is another matter.) Any project team that has worked together as a team, and that has gone through anything like the work described above is likely to have an almost embarrassing list of ideas already. This is because the emphasis throughout has been on qualitative research, the "hypothetico-deductive" scientific method, project team discussion and interpretation, judgement and intuition. The most commonly asked questions have started with "What if . . . ?"

However, there are many useful devices for helping along the process of invention. Basically, there are two sources of ideas—consumers and the company itself, particularly the project team.

1. Ideas from Consumers

It is certainly a myth that no ordinary consumers are creative; some are not, some are. Directly asking people what sort of improvements they would like in washing powder or what sort of new foods they want tends to paralyse them, particularly in single interviews when there appears to be a busy interviewer waiting for an answer. But in group discussions users of products often express a great many ideas about what is wrong with them, how they could be improved and what it would be nice to have instead of them.

It is very important that a member of the project team should sit in on the group discussions; reading a report afterwards, however perceptively it may be written, is no substitute. It is both salutary and stimulating, maybe particularly for production and R & D people, to hear consumers' comments on the company's products, to catch their tone of voice, to see their expressions and gestures. And to find out from direct experience how many ordinary people can blend sound common sense with an element of inventiveness.

One of the values of consumer group discussions is that they enable respondents to warm up, lose their inhibitions and stop answering questions in too controlled and rational a way. The "traditional" method of generating new product ideas from consumers has been, in line with this gradual thaw in responses, to move gradually from familiar areas to the less familiar and more speculative. Thus Skelly and Nelson[2] suggest starting by getting members of the group to describe their satisfactions and dissatisfactions with certain product

[1] e. g. MacDonald, E. A., " Inventing new product ideas, " *ESOMAR seminar on new product research*, November 1970.
[2] Skelly, F. R., and Nelson, E. H., "Market segmentation and new product development" (Market Research Society conference, 1966).

types or activities; then to go on to identify problem areas, by asking people to reconstruct their activities in a detailed way and to act them out, with running commentaries. The idea is that the researcher can then use these trouble spots as the core of a new product concept.

But this seems not to be going quite far enough. The other main advantage that group discussions have over single interviews is that they can become *working groups*. In other words, they have the same sort of abilities as the project team itself: the ability, by interaction, to produce more than individual members would on their own. This is, of course, particularly true if they meet more than once. It seems unnecessarily restricting to assume that the new ideas have to come by inference from what consumer group members say—they can come directly too.

The most detailed description of getting ideas directly comes in an article by Peter Sampson[1] about experiments carried out by NOP Market Research Limited. The basis of the successful experiments was people working in groups, but there were some modifications on the conventional group discussion. They became a combination of group discussion and brainstorming session. First, the members of the group were chosen as having some ability to invent ideas. Secondly, tasks were given to sub-groups—the task of inventing a new product. Thirdly, there was an element of role-playing. The results were very promising. NOP also tried a modified synectics approach on consumers, though in the time available this was perhaps not quite so successful. The short time-span of a group discussion was found to be the main problem, particularly where the product type being discussed was technical. There is of course no reason why a promising consumer group should not meet several times.

One particular device can often be valuable in group discussions— that of the "pseudo product test". In this, people are asked to evaluate an existing product which has been packed in a standard pack labelled "New formula" or "New improved". Normally they will notice differences in the "new" product, and the point is that the *way* in which people think the brand is improved can be a useful guide to the way in which they would like it to be improved. This then becomes a starting point for general discussion.

2. Ideas from the Project Team

Most of the internally derived new brand ideas will come from the project team. A suggestions scheme for the whole company, with prizes, is certainly worth having, but the experience of most companies

[1] SAMPSON, P., "Can consumers create new products?" *Journal of the Market Research Society*, January 1970.

is that its values lie rather more in goodwill, morale and internal communications than in the generation of a stream of practicable new brand ideas.

Aids to thinking for the project team are either methods of analysis or rather more simple stimuli. Here are some of them, the more analytical ones first:

(A) IMPROVING SYSTEMS

This is a matter of working out consumers' operating systems in the chosen area, either by judgement or from the research described on page 88, and asking: Which stages could be combined? Which could be improved? Which could be eliminated? Where could a new stage be inserted?

For instance, from Fig. 16 which shows a home clothes-cleaning system, ideas that could emerge this way might be: machines to do the

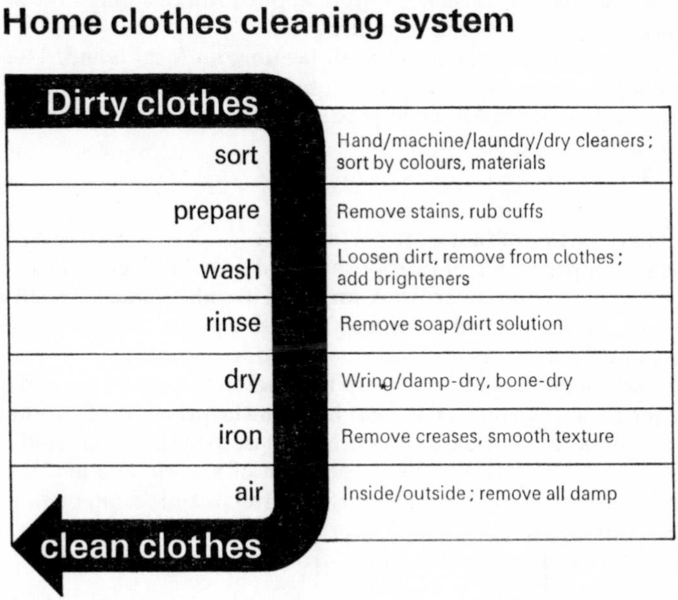

Home clothes cleaning system

Dirty clothes	
sort	Hand/machine/laundry/dry cleaners; sort by colours, materials
prepare	Remove stains, rub cuffs
wash	Loosen dirt, remove from clothes; add brighteners
rinse	Remove soap/dirt solution
dry	Wring/damp-dry, bone-dry
iron	Remove creases, smooth texture
air	Inside/outside; remove all damp
clean clothes	

FIGURE 16.

hand wash or dry cleaning and washing products to go in them; a quick dip solution to eliminate rubbing cuffs and collars; driers which enable drip-dry clothes to hang out unwrinkled; texture-smoothing solutions; grease-proof materials; ultrasonic cleaning; dirt inhibition; throw-away clothes.

This sort of approach can work too on lists of the product features in all the brands in a market and their substitutes.

(B) FORECASTING RELATIONSHIPS INFORMALLY

The starting point here is any broad set of social forecasts, unrelated to the markets being considered. One can then ask what effect each trend might have on the market. For instance, in the case of our upholstered furniture manufacturer:

Younger marriages: More working wives? More convenience needed? Vinyl upholstery? Replaceable or throwaway or reversible covers? More zips?

More teenage culture in wives? Combined seating and storage of records, junk, etc? More lying around on floor furniture, less upright?

More nomadic existence? More knockdown furniture? Blow-up furniture? Light weight furniture?

More home ownership: Central heating, no focal point? Use of walls? Storage under sitting furniture? Walls to support furniture, so no wood needed? Moulded plastics and foam? Blow-up? Folding furniture? Dual purpose?

And so on.

(C) FORECASTING RELATIONSHIPS FORMALLY

This sort of prediction of relationships and "what if?" game has been formalized into computer programs, and it is likely that we shall see more of this intellectual doodling. The value of the computer is that one can consider a great number of relationships very quickly. The Surprise Hunter facility was set up by Marketing Control Inc. originally for Pillsbury and Coca-Cola, to see if the principle of "combinatorial thinking" worked in practice. That is, to see if models could be produced to bring together extrapolation of known data and social trends with market trends, technological trends and the interaction of them. The input data of the Surprise Hunter are unsurprising; the output is surprises, which come from combining data, plus the assumptions involved.

The real value of such formal plotting is not so much that it can predict accurately as that it can surprise, and thus stimulate new ideas.

(D) INTERNATIONAL PLAGIARISM

There is nothing wrong with looking abroad. It is not only that there may be new ideas to be found directly in the US or Japan or Sweden; but also the new environment itself can act as a stimulus.

104

(E) BRAINSTORMING

This involves getting together a group of people with the express purpose of inventing new ideas. There are a few simple procedures and rules, the most important of which are that each session has a specific aim, that the ideas must come in quantity and that no idea must be turned down on the grounds that it is impracticable. Brainstorming is really no more than a way of heightening the normal interactions of the project team, but it can be useful to do this.

(F) SYNECTICS

The synectics process is an elaborate development of brainstorming.[1] In many ways it seems over-elaborate, but it can be worth borrowing techniques from it. The traditional synectics group, as described by W. J. J. Gordon, involves an extraordinarily complex selection procedure, to find six people with different backgrounds from the company. They then meet for long periods—one whole day a week for several months. They have special quarters, with library, laboratory and workshop. One can see the merits of such conditions, but it seems possible to get most of the benefits without going to such lengths. The project team is after all a mixture of skills and backgrounds; the members do have some creative ability (otherwise they would hardly have been chosen); they should occasionally take a whole day away from their normal environments; they should at times meet in workshops, factories and laboratories—not always in offices.

The synectics procedures are equally extreme, and involve having a specially-trained leader to guide the sessions. But the principles are sensible enough; they include making the strange familiar and the familiar strange, the use of free associations, role-playing, "living out" problems and analogies. Analogies used are personal, direct, symbolic and fantastic.

(G) LATERAL THINKING

Lateral thinking is a term coined by Edward de Bono[2] to describe the sort of thinking that deliberately avoids the step-by-step, deductive, logical progression from the known or from the *status quo*, which is most people's normal mode of thinking. He suggests ways of breaking up the deductive flow by the insertion of random stimuli, the introduction of an "intermediate impossible" or the deliberate challenge of agreed definitions and principles. Sometimes these methods seem a crazy way of tackling problems; but they actually do work. This is

[1] GORDON, W. J. J., *Synectics: The development of creative capacity* (New York, Harper & Row, 1961); "Operational approach to creativity", *Harvard Business Review*, November–December 1956.
[2] DE BONO, E., *The use of lateral thinking* (London, Jonathan Cape, 1967).

8

probably because most of us, most of the time, are unable to go back to the fundamentals of any situation; the very way we formulate our problems conditions the sort of solution that will emerge.

(H) CHECK LISTS
The project team might well find it worth while to make a check list of its favourite idea-stimulating devices. Some of them, derived from the authorities quoted and other sources,[1] might be:

write down new statements of the problem—each member write down a similar problem elsewhere;

draw up models (mathematical, chemical, biological, mechanical, electronic);

try different physics: gas, liquid, solid, gel, foam, paste, etc.; heat, magnetic, electric, etc;

draw analogies;

identify variables, interdependence, logical connections, systems;

work out stereotype solutions. What would the "typical German" do? What would Onassis do? The Beatles? Communists? Hippies? Desperate Dan?

browse through stimulating environments—Woolworths, Petticoat Lane, stationery shops, science museums, unlikely trade magazines, comics, etc.

pick out nouns at random from the daily newspaper and relate them to the problem.

NEW BRAND CONCEPTS

The next stage is one at which everything done so far is brought together. It produces a description of the proposed new brand or brands, with an indication of its prospects for sales and profits. Most of all it provides a written *theory of what might work*. It is not so much a plan as a working hypothesis. Normally it is best to write down these concepts in a free and discursive style, rather than cramping them into a set format, because the result should still be more stimulus than blueprint. The elements needed are a forecast of the market; a description of the new brand concept and its *raison d'être*; and a statement of the implications for the company.

1. Forecast

There are many different methods of forecasting in current use.[2] But

---

[1] Especially, EILOART, T., "Fanning the flame of innovation", *New Scientist*, 11 September 1969.

[2] CHAMBERS, J. C., MULLICK, S. K., SMITH, D. D., "How to choose the right forecasting technique", *Harvard Business Review*, July–August 1971.

it is best to think in terms of different stages of forecasting[1] and maybe to give them different names.[2] Many of the undoubted difficulties that arise over forecasts come through not being clear about which stage is being used.

The first, usually projection or extrapolation, is a matter of saying what will happen if things go on as they have in the past. Methods include putting rulers across pages or continuing curves by eye; working out trend lines by the least squares method; exponential smoothing or trend analyses. The degree of error to be expected from using the "wrong" method is usually trivial compared with the potential errors built into the basic assumption that the future will be like the past.

The second stage, prediction, is more complex, but uses much the same methods. It aims to work out a model of the forces operating on the market to be predicted, by analysis of past data. The model might show, for instance, that a market size is related in a definable way to growth of GNP, household formation, age of marriage, advertising expenditure and interest rates. These variables are projected or extrapolated, and a predicted market size worked out according to the model. This tends to be rather more accurate, but need not be.

The third stage, forecasting, is more qualitative. It is essentially applying to a prediction the presumed effects of presumed future events. It takes into account all the possibilities worked out by technological forecasts; social and political events; the possibility of substitutes, and so on. Thus it combines the vulnerabilities of predictions with those of an informed crystal ball.

It is easy to find examples of forecasting that went wrong. The UK National Plan was misleading before the ink was dry. As we saw above, most forecasts of the frozen food market were optimistic. An experiment by JWT, using Family Expenditure Survey figures, projected 1963 figures for 90 product types from 1954–59 trends. About 40 per cent were accurate within 10 per cent, but about a quarter were over 30 per cent out; and the inaccuracies were rather greater when a prediction was made using income elasticities of demand. One US study[3] suggested only a moderate ability in companies to forecast their own revenue five years ahead to within 30 per cent.

But, however inaccurate the results may be, there must be some attempt at this stage to forecast the chosen market, including of course the effect on it if the company were to launch a new brand.

[1] ZINKIN, M., *A child's guide to planning*, *Applied Economics*, Vol. 1, No. 2, 1969.
[2] DAVIS, E. J., *Techniques in market forecasting* (J. Walter Thompson Company Limited, 1969).
[3] VANCIL, R. F., "The accuracy of long-range planning", *Harvard Business Review*, September–October 1970.

2. The New Brand's *Raison d'être*

Next the nature of the proposed new brand is described. Not in detailed terms, because quite clearly they have not yet been worked out. But in terms of a *theory* as to why a new brand should succeed; what sort of brand it would have to be to succeed; what its price/quality/value relationship to competitors would be; what sort of brand share it might aim at; what it would have to do functionally; what sort of appeal it would have to have; why this company should be the one to do it; what there would be about it to enable it to command a worthwhile profit margin; what the opportunity really is, what sort of desires in whom might be satisfied by it; and so on.

3. Implications for the Company

The implications for the company can also be worked out in only a very broad way. It is quite impossible to cost accurately something that has not yet been designed, and it is only misleading to attempt to do so.

Implications to be worked out, in this qualitative way, are:

R & D: Would it mean a heavy or light R & D programme? Is there likely to be mainly basic research needed, or applied research, or engineering design? Would it mean new facilities or people? Roughly how expensive might that be?

Production: Would it mean new factory space? New machinery? New processes? Would it require a heavy investment? More people? New skills? Roughly what might the investment cost?

Marketing: Would it mean new systems of distribution, sales, merchandising, transport? Could it share existing systems? Roughly what might the new facilities and people cost?

Profits: Would it be a business with a high risk and high return, or low risk and low return? If it worked, roughly when might the break-even point be? Roughly how much initial capital would be required?

REVIEW

The planning stage ends with the first major review. Top management is drawn back formally into new brand development, and reaffirms its personal involvement in and responsibility for the end results.

The review criteria are essentially company policies. Are the new brand concepts the sort of thing that the management had in mind when setting up the programme in the first place? Are they the sort of new brands that the company should be developing?

It might seem a little strange that so simple a question has to be asked, when, after all, the company policies were the starting point for the whole programme. The fact is that the management cannot know *precisely* what its policies are until a new brand concept is put forward. It cannot set criteria in advance so clearly that it will be immediately apparent whether any particular idea fits them. Many companies have in fact tried to set up *screening systems*[1] whereby different weightings are given to different attributes scales (five for plant utilization; three for distribution; seven for technology—each operating on scales running essentially from "very difficult" to "very easy"). But it is quite impossible to work out the weightings and scales sensibly in the abstract. The screening systems merely get in the way of evaluating specific projects.

What the project team and top management have to do is go back over the arguments, theories and calculations done so far, and ask whether they all seem valid.

This is certainly not the stage for working out detailed return on investment figures as a basis for decision-making; it must be quite clear that the basic data available for doing so are far too speculative. The sort of ROI thinking to be done is very much the back-of-envelope kind—will it be large, medium or small, and roughly when? One of the obsessions of the new product development literature[2] has been the problem of deciding between alternatives, and the need for quantitative methods for doing so. In practice, any choice between alternatives is usually clear enough on the broad proposals; and if it is not, taking guesses to three places of decimals will hardly help. There is often a temptation too to call in the accountants, on the naïve assumption that accountants are dealing with an exact science; but it is much more important that the project team and top management should come to grips with the profit implications themselves.

Nor is there any case for trying to make decisions by *testing* these new brand concepts.[3] It is not completely pointless to try out verbal descriptions of new brands on potential consumers; there is always some value in finding out people's responses to a relevant stimulus. But the idea of using such tests to make decisions between concepts or to make go/no-go decisions is very dangerous indeed. The fact is that a concept and a finished brand are two very different things.

In this review, the management can go further than the project team. As well as going through the theories and ideas in a rather more objective way, it can take a broader view of constraints and it can express the wishes of the company as a whole rather better.

---

[1] ANGEAR, T. R., "Product profile analysis", *The Director*, April–May 1971.
[2] e.g. PESSEMIER, E. A., *New-product decisions: An analytical approach* (New York, McGraw-Hill Book Company, 1966).
[3] KING, S. H. M., "How useful is proposition testing?", *Advertising Quarterly*, Winter 1965/6.

There are many constraints within which the whole company is operating. The management will want to consider how the proposed new brand concepts accord with the legal framework. How do they fit the management idea of the company's social and community obligations? What are the implications for employment levels? What about patents? Gentlemen's agreements in the industry, and the dangers in breaking them? Government policy and pressures? Investment grants, etc? What dangers of a takeover, if too long-term a view of profits is taken?

Finally, as so often, it comes down to management commitment. Does the project team's idea seem interesting, exciting or stimulating to the management? Is it what they, representing the company as a whole, really want to do? Is the company capable of it; should it be made capable of it? Is it something to which they, as a management, can really feel committed? Do they feel personally responsible for it? The new brand concept may well be doomed, unless they do.

TWO EXAMPLES

This whole planning stage may seem a rather long and over-elaborate way of reaching a few new brand concepts. While it is certainly true that many—maybe most—failures can be traced to poor planning, it is not likely that any company would want to go through all the processes in as much detail as described above. To show how it can work in real life, here are two examples of how successful new businesses were planned. Like all case-histories, they seem a great deal neater in retrospect than they did at the time; but, even taking that into account, the *pattern* of planning was very close to the sequence suggested above.

1. British Bakeries: Packaged Cakes

This development really goes back to about 1960. The Joseph Rank business in the early 1950s was flour milling, and it faced strong competition in a slowly declining market. As a result, British Bakeries was formed to build up a bakery chain, partly as a means of guaranteeing outlets for flour, partly because of the economies of a more vertically integrated business. By 1960, British Bakeries had acquired a large number of regional and local bakery businesses. Most of these bakeries were selling cakes, though their type and quality and degree of packaging varied enormously. Some were almost wholly selling "tray confectionery" (daily delivery open cakes), some were making high quality, standard packaged cakes for Marks & Spencer. One of the main activities for British Bakeries during the 1960s was rationalizing this very diverse operation; it was a gradual and difficult process, since the nature of the business means that it must remain locally controlled. Against this background, here in summary are the planning elements that led to their new range of packaged cakes:

(A) COMPANY ASSETS

The company's production assets were considerable, if varied, but limited to flour and flour-based products. Marketing assets included a very large van sales force and great experience in daily delivery products, with consequent close relations with a section of the grocery retail trade. Relations with consumers were strong in one sense; any company making short shelf-life products knows very quickly and directly what is liked and what is not. But, because of the local nature of the business, there was not at that time a very great knowledge of consumers through national branding and market research. On the financial side, investment capital was available, but again the way in which British Bakeries was built up meant that there were many demands in the company for investment in plant, to improve current operations.

All in all, the analysis of British Bakeries' assets made it clear that any new operation would have to be fairly close to the existing one.

(B) TECHNICAL INNOVATION POLICY

Although there was in the RHM group one of the UK food industry's biggest fundamental research facilities, the company also had an *improver* technical innovation policy. The fact is that pioneering research in food is very long-term and uncertain in outcome. The regional structure of British Bakeries also meant that elaborate technical innovation on a national scale would have been very difficult. In practice, some of the bakery companies had led in process improvements, and this was a very good basis for an improver policy.

(C) MARKET DATA

By the time market data were examined, it was clear that the only real prospects were flour-based products. The cake market was one on the short list, and data on it came from the National Food Survey, the Attwood consumer panel and trade sources. In the early 1960s the cake market seemed to be worth rather more than £100m, and to be growing in value at about 5 per cent per annum; within it, packaged cakes were clearly growing much faster. Grocers were becoming more important outlets. There was only one major brand, Lyons; otherwise the market was very fragmented, with a fair number of private label brands. In general, quality seemed rather low, although Marks & Spencer had done much to establish higher standards.

111

(D) MARKET CHOICE

With this analysis done, the choice of *higher quality packaged cakes* was almost inevitable. They would offer more opportunities for product differentiation than bread; they would use existing skills and assets; they would be appropriate to an improver policy; the market data suggested opportunities, especially if economies of scale could be made in production. In the economic analysis, it became clear that two factors were critical, both depending on the development of the cake business through grocers. First, grocers' desire to limit the number of brands in any market would mean that any new brand would have to have a complete range of cake-types. Secondly, the short shelf-life of cakes would make a large and efficient distribution system critical to success. Both these factors favoured British Bakeries rather more than, say, Cadbury, who had entered the market in 1963.

In fact, because of the way in which the business had developed, the company went through an intermediate stage of rationalizing the existing cake output, recipes and standards, using the brand name Pandora. But in 1965, only ten years after British Bakeries had been formed, the decision was taken to introduce a new national brand of packaged cake.

(E) CONSUMERS AND CONSUMPTION

There was only a limited range of consumer research data available at the planning stage, but all of it was very useful:

(i) *Attwood panel data* were critical in showing the breakdown of buying by product type, shop type and brand. It was clear, for instance, that swiss rolls made up only a modest section of the market and that Lyons dominated it; but that "small cakes" were the biggest section and also the most fragmented. There was no major brand specializing in this section.

(ii) *Survey data*, including the National Food Survey and an Odhams survey, gave some of the basic facts on who eats cake at what meals—including the slightly surprising suggestion that adults were a great deal more important than children.

(iii) *Large-scale research* into cooking attitudes, carried out by BMRB in 1961, showed what role cakes played in housewives' lives, and the nature of the competition that packaged cakes would face from home-made (Fig. 17). It showed that home-baking, more than any other form of cooking, appealed to housewives' pride and creativity, being particularly linked with prestige and hospitality. There were signs of a trend to lighter, fancier cakes, usually made from recipes, whose visual appeal was particularly important.

(iv) *Small-scale attitude research*, group discussions and single interviews, with much use of observation as well as question-and-answer, added to this background. They established that the fundamental scale is one of home-made-ish *v.* shop-made-ish, with a subsidiary scale of modern *v.* traditional. They re-emphasized the importance of visual elements and showed that there is a regular

What housewives take into account most when making:

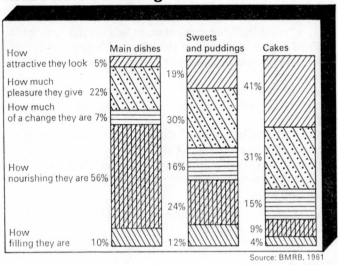

Source: BMRB, 1961

FIGURE 17. **Large-scale attitude research helped to set priorities in desired responses for the new brand**

sensual sequence used in judging cakes. First, the top is viewed as a symbol of home-madeness—it must not be too regular; next, the cake is cut, as a test of texture and freshness; finally, a second cut produces "my piece" on the plate, ready to be picked up and eaten. Success in this sequence makes the cake taste good before it reaches the mouth. Group discussions also revealed strong feelings about cakes as a treat rather than a food, and in the values of the local baker compared with the huge manufacturer.

(F) TECHNOLOGY
There was no formal technological forecasting, but it was fairly obvious, as in most food businesses, that technical developments would be a continuous series of process improvements, rather than a sudden change to new technologies.

(G) IDEAS

There were some housewife group discussions and some brain-storming. Recipe books and women's magazines were a good source. There is absolutely no problem in generating new ideas in packaged cakes.

(H) NEW BRAND CONCEPT

The new brand concept emerged fairly clearly from all this data, from the interaction of the factors considered and from a great deal of discussion. The new brand was to be:

(i) a "complete" range of cakes, to be available nationally;

(ii) of higher quality than the norm, although not initially of higher price; aiming ultimately to be non-standard, with reasonable margins;

(iii) concentrating on a small number of production units, to get economies of scale; making maximum use of the company's distribution;

(iv) concentrating on small cakes, because of their importance in the market, the scope they offer for innovation, the opportunities for process development, the opportunity for brand specialization, and thus profitability, their role—more than other cakes—as treat rather than food.

How this new brand concept was developed further is dealt with in the next chapter (page 125).

2. Dunlop Adhesives

The development of the Dunlop range of consumer adhesives in many ways involved less complex decision-making, and much less market information was available. But the sequence of planning was much the same as with British Bakeries' packaged cakes.

In 1967 the Dunlop Chemical Products Division was marketing polymers, latex compounds, selants and industrial adhesives, mainly for the motor, footwear and building industries. Because of pressure on profit margins with these products and the need to build up a larger base for operations, management decided that the Division must get into a consumer market. There were several possibilities open, and the object of the planning stage was to decide which was the best opportunity and how to set about exploiting it:

(A) COMPANY ASSETS

The main assets were the existing production facilities and the existing industrial products; great expertise in polymer technology; and a company name which was much respected by the consumer. The main weakness was that the Division had no retail sales organization and no experience of consumer marketing.

(B) TECHNICAL INNOVATION POLICY

The Division had a very strong technical department with some eighty people, responsible for development work. Basic research was done by the Dunlop Group. The need for speed more or less ruled out a pioneer policy in the early stages. (Indeed, although an improver policy was adopted, in the event the original products launched were little more than "me-too"—a major weakness.)

(C) MARKET DATA

Retail audit data, desk research and trade information established that the adhesives market was fairly small but growing; and that the consumer markets for the Division's other products were barely formed at all. The adhesives market was very fragmented. One of its features was that most of the consumer products were spin-offs from specialized industrial products. Each had been designed to suit specific materials, such as decorative laminates, or specific jobs like bonding fabrics or wall tiles. However, in the translation from industry to consumer, there had been relatively little attempt to design products that were easy for amateurs to use. It seemed likely that the specialization would continue, with the development of new materials for the do-it-yourselfer. Meanwhile, it was clear that each area of specialization tended to have a different brand as clear leader—Evo-Stik in contact adhesive, Copydex in latex, Araldite in high-strength epoxy resin.

(D) MARKET CHOICE

The choice of the adhesives market was fairly obvious. All the other possibilities would have needed technical pioneering and considerable consumer education. For a company which had to set up a retail organization from scratch and which needed rapid results, this would have been taking on too much.

(E) CONSUMERS AND CONSUMPTION

The only consumer research available was small-scale and qualitative. The main thing it indicated, very strongly, was that do-it-yourselfers were extremely confused about the different sorts of adhesive and what should be used for which. The retailer therefore had a very strong influence on the buying decision. Do-it-yourselfers' current behaviour and attitudes would not necessarily be a very good guide to what might happen in future.

(F) TECHNOLOGY

There was no formal technological forecasting, but it was recognized that adhesives are the sort of product which could change quite considerably in technology. There was clearly scope for improvement in most adhesives, and it was probable that some pioneering research would ultimately be needed. In the immediate future, developments in consumer adhesives would probably be slower than in industrial.

(G) IDEAS

Ideas for new types of adhesives came from brainstorming sessions at the advertising agency; project group discussions; information from the US; analogies with industrial products. In the event, at this stage, the need for speed ruled out many ideas for technical improvements, and most of the new ideas that were in fact used were for improved packaging and application methods.

(H) NEW BRAND CONCEPT

The critical factors in the market seemed to be the degree of specialization by brand and purpose, and the importance of the retailer. Because of the existence in industrial form of Dunlop products that covered

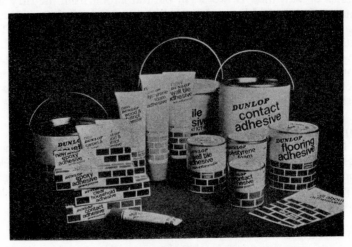

FIGURE 18. The new brand concept was an integrated
range of specialist adhesives

some 90 per cent of consumer uses, and because of the company's strength in the *general* reputation of its name (unlike the major competitors), the new brand concept was a range of specialist adhesives rather than a few broad all-purpose products. (ICI tackled the

116

market the other way, producing an all-purpose adhesive, Dufix.) This rationalized approach to all glueing needs would also offer distinct advantages to the retailer.

Because of competitors' weakness in this respect and because of the initial "me-too" nature of the products in the range, the new brand concept concentrated a great deal on offering improvements in the whole area of the use of adhesives—that is, the products plus information about them plus aids to using them. The new range aimed to offer for each product something that made it a little bit easier to use—a new sort of spreader, a way of avoiding spillage, and so on.

The Dunlop operation was a very ambitious one; moving from industrial products to a consumer brand is not easy. The very speed needed led directly to several problems. One of the values of going through the planning stage so methodically was that the company went into the developmental stage with a realistic view of the prospects and a clear set of objectives.

5 *Development*

In many ways, the development stage is the one most critical to the new brand. And yet it is the one in which a book can help least. That is because this is the most fundamentally creative stage, and there is a limit to which creativity can be helped by method. What can be done is at least to establish the principles and set the framework in which creativity is likely to flourish.

Again, it is a matter of going back to the theory of the successful new brand.

If it must be above all a *totality*, then the physical product and the communication elements must clearly be linked together by a common set of objectives; they must clearly be developed together and tested together. Not, as so often happens, one after the other.

If it is to be relevant to people's needs or desires, its starting point and language must be in consumer terms; and if it is to be unique and salient, tests must be designed that are not automatically weighted to safe majority views or to past values.

Fig. 19 shows a pattern of work that takes these requirements into account. It starts with a preliminary statement of creative strategy—set in a form that will be meaningful for designing both the physical product and the communications. Next, the product and the communications are produced to meet the strategy, with a great deal of discussion between the two lots of people responsible. Next, each is rather roughly tested, to see if it does in fact achieve its part of the strategy. Then the two are brought together into the first prototype new brand. That is tested, partly to check it against the strategy, partly to see whether as a totality it seems to be relevant to people's wants and to be interesting and desirable. What is learnt from this test feeds back, to modify the creative strategy and/or the product formulation and/or the communications. From these modifications another

Development stage

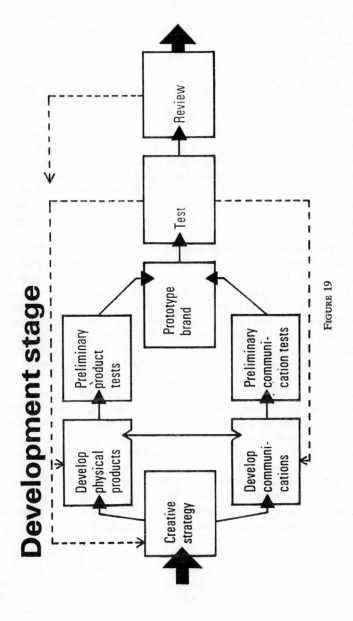

FIGURE 19

prototype new brand is produced (usually without further separate tests of the elements) and is tested. The process goes on until the evidence suggests that a new brand has been created that is worth progressing further. Finally there is another review.

There are several reasons why real life is rather less neat than the flow chart suggests.

There has to be a whole set of compromises between the ideal solution and the means of reaching it. For instance, there is no doubt that all the elements of the brand interact, and thus to test them separately could be very misleading. On the other hand, if we do not attempt to make some assessment of the elements separately, we cannot tell what should be changed to make an improvement. Again, there is the problem of the circularity of setting the target group. If we cannot know the ideal target group for the new brand until we have invented it; and if we cannot develop it adequately unless we can test it on the proper target group, then someone has to make a judgement to break into this vicious circle.

This is the stage above all where preliminary theories and preliminary strategies have to be set out, with the full intention of modifying them later. To some people, it might seem wrong to alter the creative strategy, just because the technicians and the communicators do not seem to be able to meet its demands or because someone has a slightly different idea when the physical forms emerge. But this strategy is just a starting point; it cannot be definitive. It is just as much a hypothesis as the creative treatment.

The use of research is not too clear cut either. Its main function may be to test creative work against its original objectives, but it cannot work purely within this closed system. It must to some extent indicate whether the end result will be effective; that is, it must be partly predictive. On the whole research is most valuable at this stage as an aid to *improving* new brand prototypes and a stimulus to new ideas, rather than as an aid to decision-making. But of course there are inevitably elements of both.

The whole stage may seem unsatisfactory too in that it cannot be timed with any great precision. This is not because one cannot ask creative people to work to a timetable. It is because it is impossible to tell in advance how many times the basic feedback will have to be done to get it right. For most packaged consumer goods, it is not a particularly lengthy process. For certain simple food products, for instance, it might take only three months to go from setting creative strategy to the prototype brand test, and perhaps six weeks for each feedback, modification and re-test. Yet it is all too common to hustle through this stage in order to keep to some arbitrarily set timetable. Companies that will philosophically accept an extra delay of six months in the delivery of a new machine will resent an extra six weeks added to the stage that could make the biggest difference between success and failure—the central activity in the invention of the brand. It is a very short-sighted attitude, based ultimately on a misunderstanding of the nature of invention and of brands.

CREATIVE STRATEGY

The setting of the creative strategy for the new brand is of critical importance, even though it is a preliminary strategy and may be modified later. It acts as a brief for the R & D men and the production men who are particularly involved in designing the physical product; and for the communications and marketing people who are particularly involved in designing names, packs, advertising, merchandising, added services, distribution and so on. It also acts as a set of criteria against which they can evaluate what they have designed. Unless it is written down and understood and agreed by all concerned—and this should mean that it has been contributed to by them all—the chances of producing a coherent new brand rapidly diminish.

One cannot be too dogmatic about the precise form that this creative strategy takes; people and situations vary. But the approach suggested here has the merits of being clearly based on new brand theory and of working in practice. There are four headings under which the strategy is laid out:

(A) TARGET GROUP
This is the section which is most likely to be modified in the light of development and testing. In the end the new brand may have a really strong appeal to only a segment of the population, but we may never be able to identify the segment except in terms of the brand itself. So setting the target group must be done in rather broad terms at first, preferably linked to people's relations with the market and their behaviour and attitudes towards competitive brands. As work proceeds, progressively more people will be eliminated until the target group becomes more precise.

On the other hand, the creative people who have to invent the product and the communications will be much more stimulated and given a much better sense of direction, if they have a fairly clear-cut stereotype in mind right from the start. This is where the compromise comes in. Probably it is best first to set the target group in broad terms, mainly for the purpose of calculating the number of likely prospects in the market and for drawing samples of consumers on whom to test prototypes; then to describe a stereotype group of consumers, in more evocative terms. There will still be an element of circularity. The

121

stereotypes cannot be fully described except in terms of their responses to brands, and their final description will depend greatly on the sort of new brand that the designers produce.

(B) TARGET RESPONSES: SENSUAL

This is a statement of the desired sensual responses to the new brand. That is, the ways in which it is to appeal to the target group's senses of sight, hearing, taste, touch and smell. What in particular do we want the target group to notice about the new brand? Again, this is most usefully set in relation to other brands in the market, if we are considering a formally defined market, or to substitute products, if we are considering a new type of product. The key points of difference may of course be in any sensual dimension of the product, but the creative strategy must certainly contain a reference to where the new brand should be positioned on the fundamental scales that emerge as most important from the product tests at the planning stage (page 89).

These desired sensual responses are clearly of particular importance to the R & D and the production people. The structure, design or formulation of the physical product will obviously have the major effect on how people perceive it sensually. But it is important to communications too—the style of a pack will always affect what people notice about the contents. For instance, in one recent test the cigarettes from a very dark pack appeared to be so strong that they actually made smokers cough, despite the fact that the cigarettes themselves were unidentified samples of the brand regularly used by these smokers.

The important thing about this part of the creative strategy is that it is set in terms of the consumer and his *responses*, not in terms of input. In effect, it says to the R & D man that it is his job to create the formulation, through his technical and creative skills; what matters is not so much what goes into the product as what effect it has on the target group. It is not a conventional design brief, the sort that lays down a formula or technical performance criteria. The R & D man has to create that sort of brief for himself, or more probably a series of such briefs, as his hypotheses about how to achieve the creative strategy.

(C) TARGET RESPONSES: RATIONAL

In just the same way, the creative strategy sets out a list of desired rational responses—what the target group should believe about the new brand. Again, it is a matter of setting priorities, picking out those beliefs that will most clearly set the new brand apart from competitors and make it seem more desirable. Picking the right priorities partly derives from reviewing the research from the planning stage in a green-fingered way, partly from creative judgement. The objectives must on the one hand be ambitious, because no unambitious new brand is likely to succeed. On the other hand, they must be realistic; it is no use asking for perfection on all rational attributes. This sort of dilemma is why the creative strategy has to be provisional at this stage; nobody knows exactly what could be achieved until they have a try.

The desired responses at the rational level are usually concerned with the structure or ingredients of the physical product; its function, performance and purpose; and sometimes with the people who use it. It is a matter of selection of the critical attributes, translated into users' terms. For instance, a desired belief might be that the new brand contains a special ingredient to bring out the flavour; not that it contains monosodium glutamate (which may or may not be the best means of achieving the belief). Or that a new brand of twist drill is specially designed to go through masonry without becoming blunt; not that it has a tungsten carbide tip (there might be some better sort of tip).

There is a shared responsibility for both setting and achieving rational responses. On the one hand, the R & D and production people are particularly concerned with designing to meet objectives of structure and performance in products. On the other hand, the agency designing advertising and packaging starts from the consumer's existing patterns of belief, and tries to see what elements in structure and performance will best sustain the beliefs. The two approaches do not necessarily meet in the middle. For instance, lather in washing powders is, from the technician's point of view, of very little importance in functional efficiency. However, housewives have always used the amount of lather as an indication of efficiency, probably because it is the only way in which they can see the powder working. It is unlikely, at the moment, that a washing powder without a lathering ingredient could get consumers to believe in its efficiency—irrespective of laboratory tests. In other words, any belief will depend partly on "actual" performance, partly on how it can be explained.

One element of desired beliefs must nearly always be tackled—that of price, price range or value for money. Should the new brand be believed to be better than competitors at a higher price, better at the same price or just as good at a lower price? It is partly a matter of the actual price, and the limitations imposed by that; partly a matter of observable functional or performance differences; and partly a matter of the spirit of the new brand, which relates more to its emotional appeal.

(D) TARGET RESPONSES: EMOTIONAL
Finally, there is a description of what we want the target group to feel towards the new brand, at the emotional level. What are its nature, style, associations, personality and tone of voice to be? What are the

psychological rewards of using it, serving it, giving it, receiving it? What is it to communicate between giver and receiver? It is certainly the hardest part to set down and to follow, because language is limited in the area of emotional response. It is here above all that it will be necessary to adapt the strategy as a result of creative experiments. It is very likely, for instance, that a successful pack can explain to the strategist much more clearly what he really meant than his own written strategy did.

There are some implications here for R & D and production. For instance, the desired emotional responses to a new toilet soap will affect decisions about shape, size, texture, colour and style of perfume. But on the whole, it is the communications that will most affect the appeal to the emotions.

Perhaps most important of all will be the desired personality for the brand, because it is this above all that can link the diverse elements of product and communications into a coherent whole.

This simple way of laying out the creative strategy for the new brand should be thought of more as a philosophy than a rigid format. The important elements are, first, the deliberate selection of targets and, secondly, the expression of these targets as consumers' responses —what should result from the new brand, not what should go into it. Setting new brand design objectives is never going to be easy. But, accepting that, this method does have four very important advantages.

It translates the design objectives into the only common language that can link all the different elements—the language of the consumer and what he wants from a new brand. Thus it can play a big part in bringing the project team together.

It gives the fullest scope for creativity on the part of all the designers, because it tells them what results have to be achieved; it does not limit them by telling them what to do. This creativity is essential if the new brand is to seem really new and stand out from the crowd.

It is a way of taking into account the full range of appeals of a new brand, all the satisfactions that it might give—not just the functional ones.

It results in a clear set of criteria for evaluation of results by the use of consumer research. If the design task for the new brand is to get certain responses from certain people, then the research job is to ask the question "Does this new brand prototype get these responses from these people?"

The individual members of the project team can then derive from the brand creative strategy those elements that are particularly relevant to them. These can then be translated into sub-briefs for their own working groups (for instance, the R & D team in the laboratory or the advertising agency account group). Where this is to be a range of new products, there can be a further stage. First, a strategy is set for the range as a whole, which will govern not only the style of all constituent parts but also what lines are to be put into the range. Then, if necessary, each one of the lines can have its own creative strategy too.

As a very condensed example of this, here is a summary of the first creative strategy worked out for British Bakeries' new range of cakes:

(A) TARGET GROUP

The broad target was simply all housewives who were currently buying the main brands of packaged cake. That is, as a starting point and for the purpose of drawing samples for research, the people to be eliminated were housewives and others who were not buying packaged cake. This meant setting aside, at first, the distinct possibility that a new brand would bring in some new buyers of the product type; and also setting aside the housewife's family. The important thing about setting the target group at this stage was to keep out people who might "contaminate" the research findings; whatever the probability that a small number of non-buyers of packaged cake and the buyers' families would influence choice, the central part of the target group would be the housewives already in the market. And the housewife's attitudes to the cakes as both eater and server would be critical.

The stereotype target group could go rather further than this, and pick out those people who were not satisfied with the general quality and presentation of "shop" cakes, and wanted something rather better; who were prepared to be self-indulgent and did not feel guilty about serving bought cakes; who wanted a bought cake to be as exciting as a home-made cake. This sort of description of the target group was clearly more useful and stimulating to creative people; equally, it was clearly not a practical one for drawing samples of people for research.

(B) TARGET RESPONSES: SENSUAL

The cakes, packs, advertisements and display material for the new range aimed as first priority to get the right sensual responses, particularly recognizing that taste perceptions would depend greatly on visual responses.

The strategy specifically stated:
"We want people to go through a regular sequence of
(i) top and outside of the cake—a home-made, uneven appearance;
(ii) the cut piece of cake—light and moist texture;
(iii) superb taste."

125

The emotional responses to the new brand and its personality were recognized as giving perhaps the greatest opportunity for brand differentiation. Although the range could include some new types of cake and although general quality could be better than the norm in the market, there were clearly limits to which its functional appeals could be noticeably different from those of major competitors. The strategy here included:

"We want people to feel:

(i) the nature of the brand: warm, friendly, personal, conscientious;

(ii) the basic appeal: adult self-indulgence, a treat rather than a food;

(iii) associations: people who prefer high quality and traditional standards, in a modern setting."

(D) TARGET RESPONSES: RATIONAL

The desired responses at the rational level derived very directly from the new brand concept, and from what it was that this particular company had to offer. They included:

"We want people to believe:

(i) that these are cakes made by a specialist cake firm;

(ii) that they are made by traditional methods to modern standards;

(iii) that they contain good quality ingredients and the right total recipe, not just one 'magic ingredient' (like butter)."

This particular creative strategy was an intermediate one. It was written down in this form only after some experimentation with packs and names and cakes; it did not lead directly and logically to this first creative work. On the other hand, it was written down long before the final range and specific cakes and communications were worked out; and thus did greatly help in co-ordinating and directing design work. Equally, as time went on, some aspects of the written strategy were modified in discussion, and different elements were emphasized for different lines within the range. But the fact is that the main elements of the creative strategy are as relevant to the brand today as they were when it was written, in 1965. How the pack, advertising and name were designed in line with the strategy is dealt with on pages 133–7.

DEVELOPING PHYSICAL PRODUCTS

By the time a company has reached the creative strategy stage, a great deal of progress will already have been made towards developing the new physical products—even though no experimental work has been done. This is because there has already been a lot of planning; putting forward theories; forecasting technical developments in the chosen area; analysing competitors' products; interacting with other sides of the company; playing around with ideas. All the experts on R & D suggest that these are necessary activities, and that thinking time is rather more important than sheer number of experiments.

More specifically, three activities have taken place that are usual elements of a development and design exercise. First, a project team has been set up in the R & D department. This is a satellite to the new brand project team and chaired by the R & D member of it. Secondly, the relevant literature has been searched. Thirdly, relevant technologies have been studied and their development forecast.

One further stage of analysis can be helpful. That is to list the various dimensions that have emerged from consumer research as important, and to try to relate to them various product dimensions—ingredients, interactions, relationships, functional features and so on.

After that, it is a matter of invention. The dimensions must be juggled and relationships changed, in line with theories about what would lead to improvements in the desired responses set out in the brief.

There is a series of experiments, whose results are evaluated either by judgement or by laboratory performance tests and in which the unexpected often leads to new or modified theories. Initially these experiments would be done without too many limitations but, as they become more refined, the realities of the creative strategy in terms of price/value would be taken more into account. An experiment with a higher-priced ingredient or component might be very revealing, but ultimately its findings would have to be related to the sort of price envisaged for the new brand.

The end result would be a number of samples or rough prototypes which aimed to meet the appeals of the brief. Inevitably each would be some form of compromise or balance, since in most manufactured products improvement in one element or dimension tends to be at the expense of another—particularly under cost constraints.

Although the results depend mainly on the R & D men's creativity, there are three special relationships which may help the inventive processes.

(A) R AND D AND COMMUNICATIONS/MARKETING MEN
Many of the functional features in brands are as valuable for what they communicate about the brand as for their functions. J. B. Stewart's exhaustive analysis of functional features in eight consumer durable

markets[1] showed that they were very freely used in advertising; that there was a steady rate of introduction of new features, apparently not related very much to research expenditure, and that there was a fairly rapid rate of copying by competitors in the more dynamic markets. His conclusion was that new features can do more towards building a brand's reputation than words alone, and have many incidental advantages, in their effect on salesmen and retailers and in creating unexpected publicity.

This would be taken for granted today by most marketing men, and yet there is often relatively little attempt to bring together the communication people—usually advertising agency people—and the R & D men, who are inventing the functional features, at a stage when it can really make a difference. There has to be a continuous dialogue between them, not just an occasional formal meeting; otherwise they will be too ignorant of each other's areas or too shy of each other's skills to make practical suggestions.

There is one particular problem in which this relationship can help—that of translating consumer language and desires into functional or formula terms. This is a constant difficulty, when technicians use a word in its technical sense and consumers use it in a generic or vague or even rather different sense. There is a constant problem, for instance, of relating laboratory tests to real-life conditions, and these may have their own language problems. People do not, for instance, use washing powders in controlled conditions at home; the amounts they use may vary, the way they follow instructions may vary, and what they mean by "scum", "lather", "clean", "gritty" and so on may be quite different from what the technician understands. People's main word for discriminating between, say, two brands of cheese biscuits may be "tasty"; but their use of the biscuit may suggest that it is acting mainly as a vehicle for cheese or butter or a spread, and that thus the important discriminating dimensions are not flavour, but saltiness and texture. It is only by exposing himself to the marketing or communications men, or by listening directly to consumers at group discussions, that the R & D man can really start bridging the gap.

This sort of dialogue played a vital part in the development of Dunlop's Thixofix, a new type of contact adhesive. Contact adhesives were developed mainly for bonding plastic laminates, like Formica, to wood; they give a regular and positive bond without the need for pressure. The special feature of contact adhesive is that when two surfaces are coated with it, allowed a brief period for hardening and then brought together, an immediate and powerful bond is produced.

[1] STEWART, J. B., "Functional features in product strategy", *Harvard Business Review*, March–April 1959.

While do-it-yourselfers have found contact adhesive very effective in general, research showed that they had a lot of minor criticisms. Some found it difficult and messy to apply. Some said it hardened too slowly for use on small areas; others said it took too long to spread on large areas. It was thought to be smelly; wasteful; inflammable. Many were worried about the instantaneous nature of the bond: the laminate had to be positioned accurately first time, or an expensive material might be wasted. These are the sort of snags that might not be very important for the original industrial users of contact adhesive, but they were quite disturbing for the amateur who uses it only occasionally.

It was this use of consumer research and the discussions between R & D and marketing that enabled Dunlop to look at contact adhesives from the consumer's point of view. They quickly found that his needs, especially in application, were rather different from industry's— even though many of the same words were used to describe them. It was clear that it would not be possible to produce a new adhesive improved in every dimension, because in adhesives (as in most products) improvement in one dimension often causes problems in another— or as Dunlop put it, each tends to have a pernicious contrary. The new product would have to be the best blend of attributes, and there was a vast number of possible permutations. It was only through the R & D/ marketing dialogue that they could have been reduced to a reasonable number; to have tested them all would have taken far too long and cost too much.

Ultimately four combinations were developed in the laboratory and tried out on do-it-yourselfers; one of them was almost unanimously preferred. The end result was Thixofix, a thixotropic contact adhesive in a round (paint-type) can, which spreads easily and smoothly; and while it gives the essential powerful bond, it also gives the user some valuable slideability. Thixofix had an immediate success in the market. It is hard to imagine it coming into existence at all, if everyone had stayed rigidly inside his own department.

(B) R AND D AND PRODUCTION MEN

Many manufacturers have experienced terrible problems in transferring a product from laboratory to pilot plant and from pilot plant to full-scale production. A lot of the difficulties may be inevitable, but they can at least be minimized by a close relationship between the R & D man and the production man on the project team, and between their sub-groups.

(C) R AND D AND PATENTS

It will be at this stage that the company may file its provisional specification and patent application, usually at the R & D man's suggestion. It is hard to be more specific than this, because the patent situation differs greatly from market to market. In capital-intensive industries, like chemicals, or industries where there is heavy R & D expenditure, like pharmaceuticals, it is often only the protection given by patents that makes a new brand worth considering at all. But in many industries, possibly most, patents and patent applications are a long-drawn out and costly affair that brings as much inconvenience as advantages. The patent laws were originally designed to protect inventors, encourage research and reward those who took risks to make important new advances; they were intended to be workable and useful, and were admirable in intent. Unfortunately, novelty is hard to define, and the vast majority of patent applications today are concerned with fairly minor modifications. For instance, in the electronics business it has become the practice to try to cover every variation, however trivial, in circuit design. It has become almost impossible therefore to design a piece of electronic equipment today which does not infringe some patent somewhere, more likely several. But as it is a relatively easy matter to redesign any part that is disputed, and as all manufacturers are in the same position, there is not much legal action; just a lot of unnecessary trouble.

Unsatisfactory as the present situation may be and even if, as is often the case, patents are easily circumvented in the particular markets involved, the R & D man will be wise to put in patent applications wherever feasible. At the worst, they might act as ammunition if the company is itself charged with infringements, and they are usually a deterrent to competitors. The main thing is to get priority by being first to file a preliminary application (a Provisional Specification). This gives a period of fifteen months' grace before a Complete Specification has to be filed; to be valid, the process patented must be workable and be genuinely novel and inventive. The Complete Specification sets out a full description of the invention and the nature of the monopoly that is being sought. It must include both broad and specific claims. If they are too broad, they will be turned down as unreasonable or as infringing other patents. If they are too narrow, then competitors will be able to get round them very easily.

This whole area has become a jungle of semantics.[1] The only way out is for the R & D man to be in close contact with the company's patent agent (or patent department, if there is one).

DEVELOPING COMMUNICATIONS

The communications for the new brand are developed at the same time

[1] The best simple description is WHITE, T. A. B., JACOB, R., *Patents, trade marks, copyright and industrial designs* (London, Sweet & Maxwell, 1970).

as the physical products. The processes are very similar to those for designing new advertising and packs for an established brand. But there are three quite important differences.

First, there is a much greater need to maintain close contact with the project team and the R & D man in particular. On the whole, it should be the communications man (normally an advertising agency man) who initiates the discussions on the meaning of consumer language and the right stream of "promotional" product features. This is partly because he is rather closer to the market-place, and has probably been more deeply involved than the R & D man in analysing people's attitudes and setting the creative strategy. But it is also because his creative job is much more flexible than the R & D man's; it is quicker and on the whole easier to invent a series of new communications than a series of new formulae or product designs. For most companies this would involve a fairly radical change in the way that advertising agency people operate, in their relationships with members of the company, in the way they are paid and so on. It is difficult for many companies to accept the idea of an outsider working, on terms of equal status, within a company new brand project group. But it is just as hard to imagine the company being able to provide a sufficiently wide range of communication ideas and skills within its own resources. Unless this dilemma is solved, the link between the product and the communications of the new brand will never be satisfactory.

The second difference is related to this. The job of designing the new communications is much wider in scope than for a going brand. This is because, particularly for consumer products, communications play the main part in creating the brand personality, which synthesizes and illuminates all the separate elements. That is, the new brand tends to come to life as a totality first through communications, particularly through its pack.

Thirdly, there is a much stronger argument for putting the design of all the communications in the hands of one organization. With an established brand, it is often possible to get a coherent result despite splitting up the various communication elements among various experts—advertising agency, pack design house, promotions designers and so on. This is because they are all co-ordinated by the existing reputation and physical nature of the brand. If in addition they are well briefed, the results can be reasonably consistent.

With a new brand, these controlling elements are simply not there. It is hard enough to set up an organization that will effectively blend the different elements into a totality, even when there is only one communications man in the project group. To try to do it with three or four is asking for trouble.

Pack Design

In many consumer goods it is the pack that most of all expresses the brand personality, and that is thus the best place to start designing the new communications. It is not of course always so. Canned goods, for instance, have packs so dominated by the nature of the can that relatively little can be done by surface design to express the values of the brand; in which case it might be better to start on the advertising. Equally, for durables or industrial goods, packaging has a much more functional role, and it is advertising that does most of the communicating.

For all types of product the pack does have these two different roles. In its *functional* role, the pack has to protect the product, prevent it from spilling, spoiling, breaking or getting dirty; it may have to help the use of the product, by easy-opening or metering devices; it may even be an integral part of the function of the product, as in aerosols or Paddawax or Oven Pad. In its *communicating* role, the pack has often to convey a great deal of complex information (as with the washing instructions on soap powder packs); it may have to link many diverse products into one range; it has to establish the brand as unique and immediately desirable; and it has to get as many as possible of the desired responses set out in the creative strategy.

Since the pack has to do all these things, usually within strict cost limits, and since the two roles are sometimes in conflict, it is clear that pack design is one of the most important jobs for the project team as a whole. It requires very close co-operation between production, R & D and communications men. The danger of going to an outside pack design company is that, not having been deeply involved in the whole new brand development, the designer will work mainly to "pack design values", such as colour, shape and ease of reading. He will be trying to produce a pack whose main object is to stand out on the retailers' shelves; and this is also what most research companies' "standard" pack tests are aiming to measure. Tachistoscopes are used to compare packs for readability; a pack whose name can be read in one-hundredth of a second is judged "better" than one which takes as long as a fiftieth of a second. Similar pieces of machinery measure the angle and the sharpness of focus at which a pack first becomes legible. One of the results of this sort of approach is a depressing similarity of pack design, with many diverse new brands all using the same "modern" sans serif typeface. It can be established quite easily that certain sorts of typeface and certain sorts of colour contrast do stand out best, as designers of road signs have discovered. But that is no reason for designing a pack as if it were a road sign, with a family resemblance to all other road signs. Standing out on the shelves is certainly one element of the communication role of a pack—that of salience—but for regularly-bought repeat-purchase brands it could hardly be the major element. It is far more important for the pack to express the values and appeals of the brand as a whole.

Thus the pack designer must start with, and work to, the original creative strategy for the new brand. It means working very closely with the R & D man and the production man to ensure that the content and style are entirely consistent between the product and the pack surface design. It is quite possible, for instance, to design a pack that is too "good" for the product; it might thereby attract only people with very high expectations, who would then be disappointed with the product. Equally there are many pack designs which do not do justice to the qualities of the product.

FIGURE 20. **The final dummy pack, produced in 1965**

The original Mr. Kipling pack (Fig. 20) stood out from other cake packs not because it was more readable than the others (it was probably not) but because it was different from them. The handle was the most obvious difference, and to a lesser extent the use of tear-strips, but it was much more a matter of the whole style of the pack and personality of the brand. It can be traced back very clearly to the creative strategy (page 125) and indeed, by the process of feedback, it helped to modify and clarify the strategy. There is the sensual sequence—the top of the cake looking rough and asymmetrical, the cut piece demonstrating texture and moistness and "my piece". The typography symbolizes the balance of tradition and modernity, and cake specialization. The background and style suggest the essential integrity and traditional values of the whole range, while the handle makes a Mr. Kipling cake a gift or treat more than a food. The total effect not only expresses the values of the brand, but has also influenced everyone involved in the design, production and improvement of the cakes themselves. The brand has certainly affected the company's striving for quality.

Naming

The name of the new brand has many of the same communication roles as the pack, though at a much more limited level. Many of the same principles apply to choosing it.

Though there may well be features of names to which universal criteria are applicable (pronounceability in a name is rather like readability on a pack), most of the unsatisfactory choices have been the result of over-concentration on "name values". Names are often chosen from a ready-prepared list of company-owned registrations; or to have no unfortunate associations in any language (which is likely to make them meaningless in most); huge lists are prepared by a computer (presumably so that they will be untouched by human mind); tests are done on tachistoscopes. Of course, the new brand's name should be easy to pronounce and to read and to remember; and it will be a great benefit if it can be registered. But none of these is the real point.

The really important things about a new brand name are that it should be distinctive, unique and individual; and that it should suit the desired responses set out in the creative strategy. This is why the choice of name, like the choice of pack design, has to be done as part of the whole process of designing the brand. The name is an important part of the brand personality. It says who the brand is.

One particular danger in naming brands can come from trying to tell the buyer not so much *who the brand is* as *what it does*. This seems on the surface a perfectly sensible thing for a name to do, and it can be very helpful for the first few weeks of the new brand's life. But after that, when buyers have discovered what the brand does, when there are competitors with the same functional values and when success depends on repeat purchase, it can be something of an embarrassment. The brand is being presented descriptively, as a set of functions, rather than as a brand. The immediate attraction of names like Dual, Odorono and

Magicote becomes a disadvantage when competitive brands have the same functions, plus names that can have added values.

The same sort of considerations are involved in deciding whether to use the company name plus new brand name; or company name plus generic description; or new brand name by itself. There are many variations possible according to the market, the amount of advertising to be done, rate of technical change, rate of fashion or variety of change, and so on. There are often variations within a market: for instance, Rowntrees and Cadbury have followed rather different name policies. But whatever the differences of fact, the principles for choosing are much the same. Will this name make the brand seem distinctive, unique and individual? Will it (bearing in mind the amount of advertising it will get) readily be associated with the right brand personality and the right responses?

Against these two simple questions we can see the advantages and disadvantages of certain sorts of name in certain circumstances. For instance, if there is a range of products which will constantly be changing and with little advertising for individual products, then the range would need a brand name, but the individual lines would be described by their product names. Or, if a company name covers a wide range of rather different types of product, like Kraft or Cadbury or Crosse & Blackwell, then its associations could hardly be *specific* enough by themselves to give a new brand of, say, instant tea the desired individuality and responses; a brand name alone or company name plus brand name would be more appropriate. Today, when some retail chains have quite as good a *general* reputation as most manufacturers, and yet sell their own brands at considerably less, the use of company name plus generic product description is less and less likely to succeed in consumer goods.

These were the sort of considerations that led to the name Mr. Kipling. It would have been possible to use various company names, British Bakeries or Manor Bakeries or another of the company names of the Rank Hovis McDougall group. But it was felt that they would inevitably be either too generalized or unknown to the public. In addition, a name like British Bakeries would certainly not accord with the personal and specialist nature of the brand; and the values associated with flour and cakes are totally different. A range name was needed, partly because there is a rapid rate of change in cake types, since people like variety, and partly because no single line could expect to have enough advertising to establish it. One early name suggested was "Carrycakes", as a result of the handle idea. But it was fairly quickly rejected as being too descriptive. Not only would it be unnecessary (if people did not get the idea from the handle, then they probably never would), but it would get in the way of giving the brand a personality; it was too functional. The name Mr. Kipling was in fact one of those that "came in the bath"; no doubt its origins were vague subconscious associations between the creative strategy and Rudyard Kipling, Kipps, Mr. Chips. Once it had come, it quickly became clear that it related very well indeed to the creative strategy: it suggested a specialist company, somewhat traditional, giving personal attention— just what the company and brand aimed to be. Research showed that housewives were entirely ready to believe that a man could make cakes better than they did—as long as he were doing it as a full-time job; and they found the name intriguing and different.

The problem of registering names remains. It is rather like the problem of patents; many companies nowadays get relatively little benefit from registration (other than the pleasure of irritating competitors) and quite a lot of trouble. The whole business has proliferated to the point where trade-mark and brand-name brokers are growing up. The right policy seems to be much the same as for patents—to register the new brand name if it is possible (and clearly of course to abandon names already registered). But the qualifications for registration are somewhat bizarre, and it may not be possible. Names can be rejected as having "reference to character or quality" or a geographical reference or as invented words being too near to real words. In such cases, even though there is a risk, it seems better to have the right name unregistered than the wrong name registered. Once the new brand is established, it is very unlikely indeed that any competitor would want to use the name; even if he did, he would be liable to prosecution for passing off his products as another company's. It is admittedly harder and more expensive to defend an unregistered name in court than a registered name; but the risk of having to do so is really rather slight.

Advertising

The arguments for producing advertising at this stage—instead of after the brand has been invented, as is usually done—hardly need repeating here. The advertising is clearly an important part of the communication of the brand; it may be the first part of which potential buyers are aware, and it interacts with pack design, naming and functional features. It does not need to be particularly finished at this stage, but it does have to be finished enough to represent adequately the sort of advertising that will be done for the going brand. For instance, purely verbal material rarely represents the true effects of a television commercial; but a rough film or videotape may very well do so. It is important to be planning the sort of advertising that would be used when the brand is established, not launch advertising of the

136

"new, now" type; it is the later advertising that will represent the true personality of the brand.

In the case of Mr. Kipling a rough film was made at a very early stage. It became clear that, since the sensual responses were particularly important, the visual treatment must concentrate almost entirely on the cakes themselves. And since the cakes would not look so very different from competitors', where would the brand derive its personality? There would clearly be problems in showing a Mr. Kipling: would he be real or mythical? In the end, the device was used of a voice-over talking about Mr. Kipling: and the quality of the voice expressed as much about the values of the brand as what was said. This solution to one of the advertising problems was clearly such that there was no alternative to trying it out, to see if it worked. It is all a matter of balance. It is certainly prohibitively expensive to indulge in full-scale production of advertising for a brand in this very tentative early stage. But it is foolish to try to do things unnecessarily cheaply, if the cost constraints result in a rough communication whose effect is basically different from the real-life one.

PRELIMINARY PRODUCT TESTS

There are many well-known problems in designing and interpreting blind product tests.[1] In most markets they are a long way from real life. People do not usually eat things from unnamed packs or use equipment because they have been asked to do so. They do not normally taste two things in quick succession and comment on the difference. We do not really know what effect these artificialities have on their ability to discriminate, nor how much the differences they detect really matter. What we do know is that the form of the test quite markedly affects the results.[2]

There is the problem of what Kuehn and Day call the majority fallacy[3]—the idea that a product has to be preferred by the majority to be a success; problems of order effects:[4] in taste tests, for instance,

[1] PENNY, J. C., HUNT, I. M., TWYMAN, W. A., "Product test methodology in relation to marketing problems", *Journal of the Market Research Society*, January 1972.

[2] BENGSTON, R., and BRENNER, H., "Product test results using three different methodologies", *Journal of Marketing Research*, November 1964.

[3] KUEHN, A. A., and DAY, R. L., "Strategy of product quality", *Harvard Business Review*, November–December 1962.

[4] BERDY, D., "Order effects in taste tests", *Journal of the Market Research Society*, October 1969; LAUE, E. A., ISHLER, N. H., BULLMAN, G. A., "Reliability of taste testing and consumer testing methods", *Food Technology*, September 1954.

there is a marked bias in favour of the first product tasted, and while the order can be rotated to weight the results, it casts doubts on their meaning; problems of the reliability of people's discrimination:[1] some who prefer one product to another are really guessing, while some who say they cannot tell the difference may actually be able to do so; problems where an attractive first taste would become too cloying by the end of the third packet, while a product that would succeed in the long run is rejected as too unusual on the first taste; problems of people forgetting about the first product tried by the time they have used the second, of being biased in favour of anything they are asked to try or of simply getting confused.[2]

Despite all these problems, there is a real need to evaluate the various product samples that have emerged so far. They must be tried against competitors and the most ineffective ones must be eliminated. Even though the product may perform differently when tried on the right consumers in the right pack, it would normally be quite impossible to take all the test products as far as their final presentation before testing them. Even then, the tests would probably not produce results that allowed R & D men to see precisely where improvements could be made.

So there has to be a compromise. These preliminary product tests must be recognized as very far from perfect, and they should be planned to give broad guidance and stimulus, not fine discrimination. They should not be elaborate product tests with large samples; there is little point in having results reliable to one percentage point when the system as a whole is so imperfect. Indeed there is a lot to be said for the project team or members of the company or the advertising agency carrying out some of the product tests; they will not be a representative sample, but they will not be so unrepresentative that they cannot reliably eliminate some of the really hopeless product samples.

There are several uses for these preliminary product tests. First, they are a crude test of the R & D man's hypotheses—for instance, that a new product can be produced which is an improvement on the competition.

Secondly, they can narrow down limits. They may be unable to say precisely what balance there should be between two ingredients or two "pernicious contraries", but they will help to establish the ranges within which an answer must be sought.

[1] GREENHALGH, C., "Some techniques and interesting results in discrimination testing", *Commentary* (now *Journal of the Market Research Society*), October 1966; "Discrimination testing: Further results and developments", (*ESOMAR Congress*, 1970).

[2] CLARKE, T. J., "Product testing in new product development", *Commentary* (now *Journal of the Market Research Society*), July 1967.

Thirdly, they can begin to discover the numbers of people who prefer different positions along the basic scales—say, the sweet to savoury scale—and plot a preliminary distribution of these preferences. By relating these preferences to current brand use and preference and to other characteristics, the research can help in selecting samples for future research.

Fourthly, they can help to show the sort of language used about this product type and the links between language and product design or formulation.

Finally, they can help to pick out product features with promise or elements that have failed. The failures do not necessarily need large samples or majorities to comment on them. If a new electrical device gives a shock to only one person in a hundred, that is still a very useful finding.

These types of uses suggest what form the research should take. The samples, though fairly small, should be very carefully selected to be representative of the proposed target group for the new brand, which will at this stage still be set in fairly broad terms (as "all packaged cake buyers" for Mr. Kipling). A sub-sample should certainly be interviewed in some depth, either with open-ended questions in single interviews or by group discussion. The trial of the product should be designed to be as near to real life as possible, but the needs of speed and economy must be considered; this is not the place to spend the major part of the research budget. Information collected must include use of and preference for existing brands on the market. And the basic test questions must do more than simply establish preferences for the different product samples; they must attempt to find out why one is preferred, on what dimensions it is preferred and by how much. Product tests, particularly when the products are placed in the users' homes, tend to be expensive, and it is therefore wise to get the respondents to try as many different products at a time as possible. There is some danger thereby of biasing results, but there is a much greater one in limiting the number of products tested; the danger that, by the highest common factor principle, the company will only test "safe" formulations in the middle range—which is unlikely to lead to interesting new brands.

The most important feature of these preliminary product tests is that they are aiming to help the R & D man to achieve the objectives of the creative strategy. They are also to help him see in which direction to move if he has not succeeded and the range within which he must work. In other words, the tests should be essentially qualitative and diagnostic rather than quantitative and predictive.

PRELIMINARY COMMUNICATION TESTS

This is true also of the preliminary tests of pack, name and advertising. The research aims to discover whether they have achieved the aims of their designers rather than whether they will be "effective"; and if they are not achieving the responses set out in the creative strategy, why not.

Despite the promotion over the years of many special research techniques which purport to *predict* the "effectiveness" of advertisements, there has come to be a fairly general agreement recently that this is not feasible even for established brands; that the main purpose of advertising research is to help judgement to improve advertisements and relate them better to their communication objectives; and that it is only market tests that can ultimately pass judgement on a campaign, within its total context.[1] This is clearly even more true of advertising for new brands, where there are so many more uncertainties and where there are not the stabilizing factors of an established product and reputation.

Small-scale qualitative research is most valuable here, either single interviews or group discussions, or both. Most of the larger agencies are now regularly using such research as an integral part of the creative process. Again, most of the disadvantages of small-scale research—and they are not really very serious disadvantages—can be offset by a careful selection of the sample so that it includes only members of the target group. There is no reason, apart from cost, why larger samples and a rather more structured approach should not be used also, provided the sample is properly classified and the aim of the research is diagnostic. For instance, the Clucas technique has often been found to add a further dimension to more discursive research.[2] This is a technique which aims to quantify the extent to which material succeeds in conveying the ideas it is setting out to convey; it also provides valuable hints for improvement by answers to the question "The first time you saw that scene, what was going through your mind?"

In a sense, this small-scale qualitative research will be monitoring the first occasion on which consumers are faced with what looks like a real brand. Thus the material to be exposed should be whatever is judged to express the nature of the brand most fully. For most consumer products it would be a dummy pack, with maybe some supporting print material. Where there is a strong rational element in the

[1] KING, S. H. M., "Can research evaluate the creative content of advertising?", Market Research Society conference, 1967 and *Admap*, June 1967; LOVELL, M. R. C., JOHNS, S., RAMPLEY, B., "The pre-testing of press advertisments", *Admap*, March 1968.

[2] ROCHE, M., LODGE, G., YASIN, J., "A pre-test market programme", *Admap*, April 1970.

appeal, as for a new headache remedy, the main material might be press advertisements. Where demonstration of new features is likely to be important, probably a rough film.

Though this stage might seem particularly suitable for regularly bought packaged goods, because the communications are particularly important for them, the same principles apply to durables or industrial products. There may not be a pack, but the product is often its own pack. For instance, with cars there can be tests of black and white or colour photographs or even drawings of a new model; followed by tests of the clay model, which is usually full size and virtually indistinguishable from a real car on the outside.[1] Group discussions have been used successfully in the car industry for testing the communications (that is, styling) as have single intensive interviews.[2]

Since this is still very much an exploratory stage there are likely to be alternatives, presented usually as different new brands; the act of choosing helps to bring out people's comments. One valuable way of exploring is to express the new brand's personality at the extreme ends of one of the basic scales—one dummy pack might be very Olde Englishe, another very Continental and gourmet.

PROTOTYPE BRAND TEST

When the product samples and the communication materials have been modified and narrowed down, they can be put together, and the new brand starts to come to life as a totality. At this stage there are likely to be two or three alternatives, and they too may express somewhat extreme ends of one of the basic scales, to help the final positioning.

The object of testing this prototype brand is not only to continue the process of exploration and improvement but also to see how product and communication elements interact with each other; and to improve the interaction. Thus the method remains more qualitative than quantitative, more diagnostic than predictive.

Again, group discussions are the most useful type of research. By this time, it should be possible to narrow down the target group somewhat; each new piece of research is adding to knowledge about requirements in the market. It is the combination of developing better criteria for choosing members of the group discussions, and sticking to them meticulously, with the freedom of expression within the discussions

[1] LEYSHON, A. M., "Product testing in the automotive industry", *Commentary* (now *Journal of the Market Research Society*), April 1968.
[2] HORROCKS, R., *Evaluating and controlling marketing projects: The Capri story* (University of Bradford Management Centre, 1969).

themselves that can gradually refine the new brand and position it properly in the market.

One format is especially valuable, since it roughly represents the sequence in which people do try out new brands. In the first group discussion they are exposed to the dummy packs and advertising, usually having discussed their general habits and preferences in the market. Perhaps two different new brands are used, representing opposite ends of a scale, and the group is asked to choose between them. At the end of the discussion, they take away samples to try at home. One week later they return and discuss how the products lived up to their expectations, how the rest of the family reacted, whether they changed their preferences, how the products would compare with their normal brands, what sort of price they would be prepared to pay for them, and so on. There are many variations possible within this format. There can be two different physical products for the same new brand; or the different brands can contain the same product; or both can differ. Each sort of test can give new insights. For instance, when people change preferences after using two different brands at home, even though—unknown to them—the products are precisely the same, that is a fair indication that the product is not living up to the expectations raised by the pack.

One problem here is the degree of finish of the material. With many types of product it is easy enough to produce enough samples for twenty or thirty people to try at home, but for many it is not. Equally, it is one thing to produce one or two fairly finished dummy packs for exposure to a group; it is quite another to produce twenty or thirty printed or hand-made versions, particularly if the design is merely a transitional one. There just has to be a compromise. Often it is possible to photostat the pack and provide black-and-white versions for people to take away; or plain cartons or jars with a printed leaflet. The important thing, by the time they use the new brand at home, is to remind them of the original four-colour pack and give instructions for use or details about the product. With some sorts of product— cars or domestic machinery, for instance—it is often not feasible for potential users to try the prototype at home—there may only be one. In such cases, the best thing is to get them to come in separately to try it out, in some central place which gets reasonably near to normal conditions (that is, not the factory or the laboratory or the managing director's office). The discuss-try-discuss format is still valid.

FEEDBACK

When the results from the prototype brand test are available, there is a much more important feedback process than anything so far. The main aim of all the research in this part of the programme has been to relate execution to creative strategy, but it will certainly have given many ideas of what sort of thing is likely to work and what is not. Thus it is usually quite possible now to go back and refine the creative strategy; and it is nearly always possible to improve the physical product or the communications or their relationship. It is nearly always possible to be much more specific about the target group, even if it has to be expressed in rather a circular way, and to decide whether the new brand should have a broad appeal to a wide segment or a more intense appeal to a narrow segment.

Then the whole process is repeated, though usually the first attempts will not have been so wildly astray that it is necessary to repeat the preliminary tests of product and communications separately. After the creative strategy is modified, it is usually a matter of modifying the brand as a whole, followed by more prototype brand tests. Although there is a case for keeping one or two alternatives, in order to have a standard of comparison, it is extremely difficult to progress two competing prototype brands as "best"; they usually turn into a favourite and an also-ran. The process of modification and re-test may well have to be repeated, but by the end of it there will usually be just one new brand.

As the final shape of the new brand comes closer, so the group discussions can be looked at more as an evaluation and less as an exploration. It may be worth having rather more of them or semi-structured single interviews, in order to build up numbers. But this research is still to help the designers of the new brand, not to make their decisions for them. If designers listened always to consumers, and gave in to the majority view on every point, there would probably never be any progress at all. It is much more important that the new brand should bring intense pleasure to some than that it should offend nobody.

REVIEW

When the prototype new brand has finally been patted into shape, the work done so far is reviewed by top management. This is a very important review, for two reasons. First, the decisions and work up to this point, though not exactly cheap, have not involved the company in vast expense. Most of the costs have been salary costs; relatively little raw material has been used, and it has probably been made up in the laboratory or existing pilot plant; the consumer research programme has been based mainly on small samples. But from this point on, the costs escalate considerably. There may have to be investment in new factory space, and almost certainly new plant will have to be bought.

In the case of products like cars, the cost implications here are enough to break the company. Now is the time for management to decide whether to go on.

Secondly, this is the time for a more independent view. The project team will inevitably have become deeply involved with the new brand by now; the force of its personality will have affected them. It is absolutely right that this commitment should exist; the brand would hardly succeed if it did not. But it is dangerously easy to push ahead at this stage, simply because everyone is so enthusiastic. People start brushing aside hints of trouble; they ignore awkward findings; they put forward estimates that they secretly know are based on wishful thinking; they want to make up any lost time. The management has a difficult task here. It must support the project team, nourish its enthusiasm and be fully committed to the idea of the new brand. At the same time, it must stop the new brand's progress or change it in some way, if it seems likely to fail. What the management must never do is give grudging approval; it must never allow the project to continue, without taking full personal responsibility. There are only two options open to management—yes or no.

Part of this review is simply a matter of going back over the work and relating the results to the objectives. Does the new brand that has emerged in prototype fulfil the creative strategy? Does it still tie up with the company's original development objectives and choice of markets? Now that the management has at last seen *a brand*, is that brand the sort of thing the company ought to be selling? Should company policy itself be modified? Can the management visualize this new brand becoming a major new business? Does the economic analysis still seem valid? In other words, the review should cover not only the development stage but also the planning stage.

Clearly the review must also look forward. The project team can, and should, now be able to forecast reasonably accurately the capital costs of each step of the evaluation stage—plant, consumer research, advertising and promotion. The management can at least examine the capital needs, and relate them to the company's current financial situation. If successful, the review would end with approval for a fairly major series of investments.

It is also now possible to produce outline figures for return on investment for the new brand that are a little better than inspired guesswork. Now that there is a prototype new brand some progress can be made in costing it. The variables that go into the production costing, like the real cost of new machinery, the speed at which it can be run, its manning scales, the quantities involved, amount of overtime and so on, will be estimates for a long time. The same goes for the estimates of sales and selling price, but again it should be possible to make slightly better guesses now that an actual brand is involved and now that more has been learnt about the market. However rough they are, it is worth making return-on-investment calculations, for two reasons. First, while they are unlikely ever to prove that the new brand will inevitably bring in massive profits, they can occasionally make it clear that the company could never make a worth-while profit in this market with this new brand.

Secondly, they can help each member of the project team to learn the financial implications of variations in his own special area of expertise, and indeed to appreciate that the object of the exercise is to build a future business, not just sell a lot of product. And they can be helpful in promoting understanding of relationships between the elements, by providing conditional conclusions. For instance, that if that particular expensive ingredient is used, the production machinery would have to cost no more than £x per unit of output or the price would have to be y per cent above the current market leader (in which case maybe the packaging would have to be better or the unit size changed or the target group reduced in size).

If all goes well, the review ends with the management deciding that the new brand is in line with policy, that its development so far has been sound and creative, and that it looks as if it could be a worth-while business venture, with a reasonable return; and voting the necessary funds for the next stage—evaluation.

6   *Evaluation*

Whaat the project team has produced so far is a fairly rudimentary new brand. It has a physical product which was produced in a laboratory, not on a production line, a dummy pack and rough advertisements or leaflets. It has been tried out on only small numbers of possible buyers, in artificial conditions. They seemed to like it, but were never put to the test of actually buying it from a shop. All the forecasts of sales, costings, margins and selling price have been very rough.

But, however rudimentary, if the new brand has been through these planning and development processes, it will have three great assets. First, it is a coherent whole; all its elements have been planned and modified in relation to each other. Secondly, it has sprung from what the company thinks it can best do; it is not some stroke of genius that is better suited to a different company. Thirdly, it has the enthusiastic support of the top management; it represents the way that they want the company to go.

In other words, it looks as if the new brand might be successful in the market-place and it looks as if the company would be both willing and able to produce and market it effectively. The third stage in the programme—evaluation—has two primary objectives. First, it aims as far as possible to validate these hypotheses and quantify the results so far, before final decisions are taken. Secondly, it plans the actual launching of the new brand; it brings all the work done so far to a practical result.

Fig. 21 summarizes the main elements of this stage, the central part of which is a quantitative pre-test.

NATURE OF THE EVALUATION STAGE

The first object is validation, and there is certainly much that can be done to validate the hypotheses; but there are limits. There is no form

146

Evaluation stage

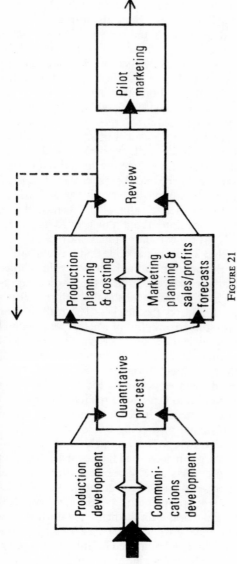

FIGURE 21

of quantitative pre-test or mathematical model which will predict the new brand's level of sales and profits with any accuracy. Many companies seem to find this rather surprising. They seem so often to hope that over-hasty or ill-conceived work at the planning and development stages can always be put right at the pre-test stage, that potential successes will shine forth and potential failures will be easily weeded out. In fact, except at the extremes, it may well be impossible to distinguish between likely "successes" and "failures" before they reach the market-place. Even then, prediction will be difficult; the test market is a fairly blunt instrument.

This means that, however desirable validation and prediction may be, the evaluation stage too should be looked on as an opportunity for experiment and improvement. In fact, there is never a time for any brand when the process of experiment and improvement can be stopped (it happens every time the advertising or pack or formula is changed); and it may be that the current set of adjustments to the new brand can only be completed when it has been tried out in real conditions. So the predictive value of the quantitative pre-test is partly one of helping decisions about how near to its ultimate potential the new brand is. At the extremes, it may show clearly that it could never succeed, or that it is so remarkable that it could hardly fail; but this is rare. What the pre-test normally does is guide choice between some experimental alternatives and help the project leader decide whether the next stage of improvement should be done before or after launching the new brand on the market. The really important predictive questions are still: Irrespective of whether we get it precisely right next year, do we think we can build a decent new business with this brand? Even if we cannot accurately predict next year's profits, do we think we have got the fundamentals right?

The second main objective of the evaluation stage—turning the prototype brand into large-scale reality—makes this rather different from the other stages. It is much more like the production and marketing planning of a going brand. Up to this point the project group has been able to work largely on its own. Where individual members of the group have used their own departments for working on the new brand, it has usually been a matter of a small departmental project group—a development group in the R & D department, a skeleton account group at the advertising agency. Now that planning for launching the brand on the market is starting, many more people are involved, and there is a greater need for setting up efficient routines and administration, a lesser need for inventiveness. From now on, the risks to the new brand are more conventional ones—muddle, cutting corners, changes in midstream, lack of commitment and poor logistics, rather than lack of inspiration.

The operation now becomes rather easier in one sense; it is a matter of fairly familiar activities, like purchasing raw materials, installing new machines, producing brochures, training salesmen and so on. But there is another sense in which it is more difficult. The detailed work involved in getting the new brand on the market must be done by people who are not nearly as involved as the project team; they have not seen the new brand through all its vicissitudes and birth pangs, and they are not committed in the same way to its success. In many ways, for them all it means is extra trouble. It is all too common for the impetus of new brands to break down at this point. Without the involvement that makes people take special pains, it is tempting for the production department, for instance, to modify the formula slightly so that machining is easier or for the salesman to relegate the new brand to last on the list, so that he can meet his targets on the main going brand.

The change from small-scale to large-scale methods required at the evaluation stage is never easy, but this is where the project team form of organization has particular advantages. The project leader is someone who is committed to the new brand and, as its potential manager, to making it into a successful business. And the project team has been made up of people only *temporarily* removed from their departments. At the evaluation stage they will be able to move back into familiar departmental roles, to manage the logistics of launching the new brand, while keeping all the commitment that will be necessary to produce enthusiasm in others.

This is also a stage in which there could be a risk of the links between the different skills—R & D, marketing, communications, production —becoming broken, with disastrous effects on the new brand and its timing. It is one thing for a project team to work very closely together; quite another for whole departments. This is where the techniques of critical path analysis are particularly valuable. They are the ideal instrument for bridging the gap between the two methods of working.

CRITICAL PATH ANALYSIS

Critical path analysis was first used in the late 1950s and its earliest successes were on a $10 million plant construction project for DuPont and on the Polaris missile. Since then it has made increasing use of computers; it has acquired a series of sub-variants, such as PERT (Programme Evaluation and Review Technique), resource summary and resource levelling; there is a substantial body of literature about it.[1]

[1] LOCKYER, K. G., *An introduction to critical path analysis* (London, Pitman, 1967); McLAREN, K. G., and BUESNEL, E. L., *Network analysis in project management* (London, Cassell, 1969); WONG, Y., "Critical path analysis for new product planning", *Journal of Marketing*, October 1964.

149

But the principles involved are simple enough. There is no need, for most new brand introductions, to get bogged down in the intricacies; and many managers have found that they have been able to add their own touches, to produce a system which suits their own particular needs.

In essence, a critical path analysis results in a network diagram of all the jobs that have to be done, in the order in which they have to be done, with the estimated time taken for each. The network diagram represents *activities* which, when completed, create *events*, which are themselves dimensionless progress points in the job of finishing the total *task*. The input to an event is simply all those things that have got to happen before it. For instance, our quantitative pre-test cannot be put into the field until questionnaires have been agreed and printed, product samples made up and packs put together. (And each of these activities can itself be further subdivided.) The important point is that the event which precedes the activity of pre-testing is dependent on the activities of at least three different departments, and if each pursues its own course without considering the others, there are likely to be delays.

In practice, most departmental managers are quite used to setting out their regular activities on milestone charts. Critical path analysis requires two further actions: the inclusion of more, smaller activities ("prepare salesman's portfolio", for instance, might be extended to cover preparing graphs, rough copy, layout, revision, final artwork, approval, blockmaking and printing); and the linking of all the activities in a logical framework.

What this inevitably means is planning the *whole* of the evaluation stage of the new brand in some detail before it starts. Actually drawing up the network is usually a good deal less complex and time-consuming than one thinks it will be. That is because the principles are simple enough; the complexity is really a matter of the amount of material to be processed, and to a large extent dealing with that is simply a matter of hard work. The normal stages would be: First, work out an outline marketing and production plan, in order to generate lists of jobs to be done (like organize exhibitions, fix distributors, train salesmen, buy plant, train operators, etc.). Secondly, break these plans down into finer detail. Thirdly, estimate the time that each of these activities will take. Fourthly, examine for interrelationships; that is, see where activity A has to be completed before activity B. Fifthly, work out just how many jobs can be done concurrently. Sixthly, draw in the critical path, the line of consecutive activities which will make up the longest time period. Again, it is less puzzling to do than describe; many of the books on the subject recommend practising on some very simple task, like boiling an egg.

The final network has a great many advantages for new brand

development, some overt and some less obvious. The most immediate advantage lies in the help given to timing the operation. If time is short, and it often is, critical path analysis can help the project manager decide which activities must be shortened or for which the normal logic must be foregone (for instance, taking action on the likely results of some research before the survey is finished). In a more general way, it can help control the whole evaluation stage; it is possible to see at a glance what is behind schedule, it makes progress reporting more purposive and makes it easier to forecast bottlenecks. It can help management also to see where time can be caught up, where a crash addition of resources will work, and so on.

In many ways, the less immediate advantages are even more important. Working out a network diagram can greatly improve the quality of planning, because it is impossible to do so without looking at the totality of the job and considering all the implications. By showing the interrelationships of activities of the different departments in a graphic way it can act as a means of communication within the company and create a greater sense of understanding and common purpose. Again, by plotting the activities and getting departmental estimates for the time they will take, the network helps to make clear who has the responsibility for each activity. Finally, and maybe most important, it can make it clear to top management exactly what still has to be done, and avoid the risk of the project group's being pressurized into skimping the work at these last critical stages, in order to bring to the market six weeks early a brand that is intended to last for decades.

PRODUCTION DEVELOPMENT

The first phase of work in the evaluation stage involves transferring production from the laboratory to real-life production machinery. This is clearly a continuum, and there are many stages of pilot plant production possible between the extremes, using mocked-up or adapted machines.

There is a very real problem here. The fact is that, whatever designers, engineers, production men or R & D men may say, there are nearly always substantial differences between a product made up in a laboratory and the "same" product made in a factory. Sometimes these differences matter a great deal, sometimes they do not; but it is very difficult to predict either the degree or the importance of the difference.

In this situation, the dilemma is clear. On the one hand, it can hardly make sense to spend a lot of time and money pre-testing a product which is different from what will ultimately be put on the

151

market. This means that the pre-test should ideally be done on products that have come off a normal production line, operated by ordinary members of the production department. On the other hand, if the pre-test is to be done on finished production-line products, the decision must already have been taken, probably some time ago, to invest in a certain sort of machinery. And if the decision has already been taken, what is the point of the test?

This dilemma is inescapable, and all that can be done is to limit its effect. The project team must recognize that it exists, must try to make the best compromise and decide what effect it will have on their interpretation of the pre-test. The direction of the compromise will clearly vary according to the nature of the production processes. If the product is a car or some form of mechanical or electrical durable goods, where laying down, starting up and running the production line can take years and cost millions, it would clearly be ridiculous to suggest that this must be done before a quantitative pre-test. The project team must clearly do its best with mock-ups and models, using the pre-test purely as an aid to judgement.

If however the product is a food produced by some grinding and mixing process, the likelihood is that a wide range of variants could be produced on the same machine. Thus the risks of wasting money and time by getting the wrong machine are less, while the risks of testing an unrealistic product are high; food products are notoriously liable to change between laboratory and factory. In this case, it would be far more sensible to do the pre-test on a production-line product.

Whatever the situation resulting from the nature of the market's productive processes, there are two fairly common-sense rules to observe. First, it is always worth working out which parts of the production line are common to a range of possible variants. The decision to buy and lay down these is more a result of the decision to go into large-scale production than of the final specification of the brand. And that decision has been made, in principle, at the end of the development stage. Thus the current dilemma may apply to only part of the production machinery; it is very important to work out what part.

Secondly, the project leader must keep a very careful eye on all the production development work. Some changes in the product are inevitable, but at least he can see that the changes are either minimal or actually improvements. The fact that a production man has been a member of the project team should have ensured that the prototypes make sense in terms of large-scale manufacture. But it is quite common for production engineers to modify the product for their own convenience, so that it fits the machinery available better, so that machine output is speeded up, because of temporary shortages in one ingredient, and so on. It would be unreasonable to expect them to have the same sort of attitudes to the inviolability of the product as the project team; and in many cases, their ideas could easily save money or improve the product. In fact, there is every reason to look for improvements and modifications here, as at other stages. The crucial thing is that everyone should be aware what changes are being made and why. It is a matter of balance. There must be the optimal improvement in production methods consistent with turning out a product similar to what has been developed and tested so far.

COMMUNICATIONS DEVELOPMENT

There is much the same sort of dilemma with the communications elements of the new brand, though the problems are slightly different. It can be an expensive and time-consuming business to produce finished four-colour packs for a pre-test, but for most brands the investment would be very small in relation to that on the production side. In any case, the pack will already have been modified several times at the development stage, and so the risk of the final version needing radical changes as a result of the pre-test is not very great. By contrast, the risk of getting a misleading result from the pre-test through using unlabelled products or unfinished packs is very great. So, in nearly all cases, it is best to use finished packs for the pre-test.

There is another problem with communications that does not really affect the production side. That is, the extreme difficulty of simulating in a pre-test the element of time and the interactions over time of advertising, packaging, word of mouth, pricing, the bandwagon effect and so on. Even if it is decided that it is worth investing at this point in a finished television commercial (and it usually is worth it), it is impossible in a pre-test to create the effect of repeated exposure to the commercial or of linking the sound and vision of the commercial with a showcard or special introductory offer in a shop. There is no very good way round this problem; the project team simply has to judge what it is that best gives the sort of communication impression that the brand will give when it reaches the market.

Two principles emerge from these problems. First, as a general rule it is worth taking the communication elements to as finished a stage as possible for the pre-test. Secondly, since pre-market conditions will nearly always understate the interactions of a market-place introduction, there can be some degree of exaggeration for the pre-test—say, a special leaflet to accompany each sample, even though it is not intended in the market-place. At the same time, of course, to make the pre-test meaningful, the communication elements should aim to present the new brand as a going concern—its long-term personality, not its short-term novelty value.

153

QUANTITATIVE PRE-TEST

The quantitative pre-test is a fairly critical part of the whole process of developing a new brand. It comes between the development stage, which is reasonably quick and inexpensive and uncommitting but very tentative, and the market-place introduction, which is almost inevitably time-consuming, very expensive and very committing. What manufacturers would dearly like to have here is a precision instrument, that will protect them from any mistakes they may have made in the earlier stages. And yet all the evidence seems to be that the pre-test does not often weed out the non-starters. Many manufacturers have found that the most commonly used sort of pre-test, the in-home product test, gives results that are either grossly optimistic or are inconclusive (in which case they are often interpreted too optimistically).

This is partly because too much is expected of them; they inevitably face most of the problems of blind product tests. It is also partly because only rarely are they properly planned. In fact, if the project team works out very carefully what questions have to be answered and the purpose of the pre-test, it can be a piece of research of immense value. To do it properly can take up a lot of time, and it is not cheap. If the money and time are not available, then it is probably better to leave it out altogether and rely on the previous small-scale research plus judgement, rather than use the results of a cheap off-the-peg pre-test for making final decisions.

The main elements of the pre-test are governed by its basic purpose, which must be mainly validation and quantification rather than prediction. This means that it will follow many of the principles of the research at the development stage, but on a larger scale.

What is to be Tested

It also affects what it is that is being tested at this stage. The questions are fundamentally about whether the new brand is achieving its objectives, rather than whether the objectives themselves were right. Thus comparisons will be between relatively minor variations of a basic new brand, not between radically different new brands. It is only a market-place test that will show which of two different new businesses will yield more profit.

What should be built into the pre-test, therefore, is a few experiments based on minor variants; and since the physical elements are nearly always harder to get right or to change afterwards than the communications, the variants will usually be in the product itself.

The Sample

The results of this sort of consumer research will always be open to considerable differences of interpretation. Its meaning will never be neat and clear-cut, and the "amateur" members of the project team are just as likely to be right about its implications as the most seasoned research professional. But where specific research skills are important is in the meticulous selection and classification of the sample of people on whom the new brand is tried. The classifications must in particular be related to use of brands or substitutes and to the basic value scales of the market involved, and to all the discriminating factors that emerged from the study of consumers and consumption at the planning stage.

The reason for this special care in classification is the need to quantify the new brand's target group. It should be clear from the development stage that some people will like the new brand, some will not; what is not clear is how many will like it or, if it is to slip into some gap, where and how big the gap might be. Analysis of the pre-test results by existing brand use or by the basic value scales will almost certainly be the best indicator of the potential scale of the new brand. If, for instance, the market is crowded and the new brand seems to be liked equally by users of each current brand or by people at each end of the value scales, then that may be a sign that its appeal is not sharp enough to break in at any point. Conversely, in a relatively new or undeveloped market, if the new brand is very skewed in appeal to one end of the value scales, it may have an over-restricted appeal.

In general, the rewards from the pre-test research will come much more from this sort of analysis than from simple totting up of scores for variant A versus variant B or from figures for the number of people who "will definitely buy" or "would switch from my usual brand". Time spent working out in advance precisely what analyses will be needed is well worth it; it can be very expensive and frustrating trying to get special analyses afterwards, once the results have vanished into a computer.

Form of the Test

The form of the test is governed by its role and its chronological place in the total programme. On the one hand, it must relate to the original objectives and the small-scale work done so far, because it is they that must be quantified and validated.

On the other hand, it should aim to have some predictive values. There must be a middle course between refusing to predict at all and relying blindly on naïve and simplistic methods (like asking people "Will you buy it?"). One of the implications of this is that the test

155

should, wherever possible, reflect *real-life conditions*.[1] This will be a matter partly of using finished products and finished communications, partly of the way in which the test is planned.

In designing the pre-test, it is worth looking back at the theory of the new brand. The three essential conditions for success were:

(*a*) it must be a coherent totality, in which product and communication reinforce each other;

(*b*) it must represent a unique blend of appeals to the senses, the reason and the emotions, as set out in the creative strategy; and

(*c*) it must be relevant to people's wants and it must be salient, standing out from the crowd. Each of these has implications for the pre-test.

(A) IS THE NEW BRAND A COHERENT TOTALITY?

Here we are really asking whether the total brand, as used in real-life conditions, coheres completely with the expectations aroused by the communications. Is there a total brand personality to which every aspect contributes?

The implication of this question is that the pre-test should be in two parts. First, we have to find out what are the expectations; then, whether the product comes up to these expectations. This two-part process represents how people do buy a new brand. Normally they hear of it or see it in the shops, and form an opinion about it before they try it. In its critical early stages, the new brand loses some potential buyers because they are simply not attracted to its personality; but much more importantly[2] it loses repeat-purchase because the original buyers do not find it is quite as attractive as they had hoped.

So the first stage of the pre-test *ideally* involves exposing the sample (normally the planned target group expressed in its broadest terms—like "all packaged cake buyers" for Mr. Kipling) to the new communications in real-life conditions, and discovering their expectations. Where this involves television—and that would be true of most new brands of packaged consumer goods—there is clearly a problem. The cheapest way of simulating exposure to television is to get people into a cinema, but it is far from satisfactory. The response rate is much lower than when people are interviewed in their own homes; the cinema has a totally different ambience from a television set; and questions usually have to be answered on a self-completed written questionnaire. The best solution is to use a mobile van which has been fitted out with a television set on which videotape commercials can be

[1] GREENHALGH, C., "Discrimination testing: Further results and developments" (ESOMAR Congress, 1970).

[2] PARFITT, J. H., and COLLINS, B. J. K., "The use of consumer panels for brand share prediction", *Journal of Marketing Research*, May 1968.

run, plus facilities for personal interviewing in reasonably relaxed conditions. Many research companies now operate this sort of mobile unit. It can get rather expensive, but if anything has to be sacrificed it should usually be the sample size rather than the method.

In this first part of the two-stage test, there would be three sorts of question. First, questions to help classify people. These would ensure that they are in the proper target group, establish their buying patterns and find out where they come on the basic value scales in the market. Secondly, after exposure to the advertising and pack, questions to discover comprehension of the pack and advertising[1] and where people feel that the manufacturer is trying to place the new brand. Thirdly, questions about people's expectations of the product inside the pack that they have seen and how it relates to other brands in the market, on the product attribute scales originally developed at the planning stage.

After these questions people would be offered a sample or two of the new brand or of their usual brand, as thanks for taking part. If there is no regular market established, they would be offered samples of the new brand or, say, three-quarters of its cash value. The proportion of people taking up the offer of the new brand would be an important indication of the number who might be prepared to try it in real-life conditions, as a result of its communications. It would of course be an exaggerated indication; the new brand would be offered free, after a deeply-involving question-and-answer session. But what it could more reliably show is how many people would *not* be likely to try the new brand in real life. Also, by referring back to the classification data and comparing the buying patterns and position on basic attitude scales of those taking up the offer and those not, it is possible to learn a great deal about the perceived positioning of the new brand; and this can be compared with people's more overt ideas about positioning.

A second value of this offer of samples of the new brand is that it can get people to try it out in a more or less real-life situation. They are *not* asked to take the new brand home to try out. They will be using it at home in a fairly normal way, perhaps influenced by a greater than usual curiosity but without the heightened attention and special exercise of critical faculties that so often spoil in-home product tests.

The second stage of the research is more straightforward. A week or so later—the timing depending on the nature of the product—the people who took up the offer of the new brand are re-interviewed. They are asked questions about who used the new brand, when, how often and so on; and what their reactions were to it. Many of the same questions can be used as in the first part of the research, particularly

---

[1] CLUCAS, J. E., "Commercial testing", *Admap*, October 1971; ROCHE, M., LODGE, G., YASIN, J., "A pre-test market programme", *Admap*, April 1970.

157

the product attribute questions. This is a rather better way of linking performance with expectation than asking direct questions, though there is no reason why the direct question cannot be asked at the end of the interview. People will have forgotten their precise answers from the first stage, and in any case will not be tempted to aim for consistency, since one set of questions was about expectation and the other about performance.

What will be generated from the two parts of the research is detailed pictures of expectations and performance, and the degree of coherence of the new brand can be seen by the extent to which these two match. It is very important that the matching be looked at by individuals rather than aggregates. It is quite common to find that the individuals who were most favourable at stage one were those most disappointed at stage two. And that is a fairly sure recipe for failure in a new brand.

(B) HAS THE NEW BRAND A UNIQUE BLEND OF APPEALS TO THE SENSES, REASON AND EMOTIONS?

It is fairly easy to see how this question can be answered by the form of pre-test described. The unique blend part of the question is a matter of studying the matching of expectation and performance; is the new brand a blend or is it a collection of unconnected bits? Is it unique or does the pattern of attitudes to it, both expected and found, seem to be just the same as to one of the existing brands? Are the potential buyers too similar to those of an existing brand?

The second element here is the question of whether the new brand does in fact have the appeals to the senses and the reason and the emotions that were set out in the creative strategy, as modified during the development stage. The sensual responses will come mainly from the second stage of the research, when the product has been tried; the emotional responses rather better from the first stage, when people will be using their imaginations more; the rational responses from both. What may be harder to establish in this sort of detailed structured research is the total brand personality; and it might be better to try to get at that by unstructured methods, maybe during pilot work.

(C) WILL THE NEW BRAND BE SALIENT AND RELEVANT TO PEOPLE'S NEEDS?

This is the most overtly predictive question for the pre-test, and thus the hardest to answer. The positioning of the new brand in relation to existing brands and declared likelihood of buying give some idea of both salience and relevance. But the circumstances are fairly artificial. It is well known that people tend to exaggerate their likelihood of buying and their liking for test brands; but the degree of exaggeration will vary according to the product field and circumstances. In other words, in extreme cases the pre-test can be confidently taken to predict failures; but it is not a very good discriminator between successes and failures in the middle ground.

The "real-life" questions are a rather better indicator. First, the proportion choosing the new brand at the end of the first stage of the test. Secondly, answers to questions about who used the brand between the two stages, how often, when, how and so on. These can give a good idea of what is likely to happen to the brand when it gets into the home. If people have been given several samples there can even be estimates made of frequency of use, which is the best guide to relevance. Again, the findings are more reliable in a negative sense. If in the intervening period only one or none of the new brand samples has been tried, then that is a fair indication of lack of interest. But where all have been used, that does not necessarily mean that the people involved would maintain their interest enough actually to buy the new brand.

There have been a number of attempts to predict success and failure more directly. Some have been by elaborate but somewhat speculative model-building,[1] with inputs based on judgement (which rather defeats the object). Others have used standard direct questions and scales, the development of norms and the relating of the norms to market-place performance. The scales have usually been very simple questions about likelihood of trial, of switching from a usual brand and of buying. It is rather like the attempts, now almost universally abandoned, to use simple mechanisms for predicting the effectiveness of advertisements. The fact remains that it is not normally possible to simulate in a single-exposure pre-test the competitive market situation, the effect of time and repetition of exposure and use. It would probably work best in a market like that of cigarettes, where the range of options for a new brand is extremely small; the only real variables appear to be naming, pack design and press advertising. In such circumstances, it is not too hard to envisage simple predictive scales being a good indicator of success or failure, particularly at the extremes (that is, indicators of failure rather than success; and in the cigarette market over the last few years, that has been a fairly safe prediction). But this is not typical of most markets. It seems unlikely that there will ever be really reliable predictive measures of salience and relevance in a pre-test.

The Cost

The sort of pre-test described here is clearly expensive. The needs for quantification and classification of the target group by brand use and

[1] CLAYCAMP, H. J., and LIDDY, L. E., "Predictions of new product performance: an analytical approach", *Journal of Marketing Research*, November 1969.

by positions on basic value scales mean that a fairly large sample must be used. In fact, the sample size required depends more on the need to compare sub-groups than on the need for a low overall margin of error; so some saving could be made by over-sampling and weighting, say, users of minority brands.

In addition, there would have to be matched samples for any variants tried out, and the matched samples would have to be big enough to produce significant differences. This implies that the experiments should be bold ones, not minor matters of judgement. The requirements for conditions nearest to real life really rule out paired comparisons.

Finally, the very form of the test, involving two parts, exposure to advertising material, recall on a named sample and extensive questions, is itself expensive.

But cutting down the cost is fairly unsatisfactory. There is little point in working with very small samples, because that has already been done, in rather greater depth, at the development stage. It is not very sensible to use the more limited traditional in-home product test, as this does not really answer many of the questions; it cannot relate expectations and performance, it is far from real life and it does not have very much predictive value. And it seems wrong to leave out the product variants since this would lose the opportunity to find out the importance of precise product specification and to use the research for improving the brand rather than as a simple insurance policy.

The quantitative pre-test may be judged too expensive and too time-consuming. That would be a pity, because its cost is usually small in relation to the potential losses of a new brand failure and even in relation to the real costs so far. Rather than trying to mount a half-hearted cheap version, it would almost certainly be better to repeat the small-scale qualitative research that ended the development stage, this time using finished packs and product.

Other Forms of Test

There are several other forms of pre-test that can take place at the same time as the major consumer survey. First, it seems worth trying out the brand on the people involved in the distributive system—salesmen, transport men, distributors, agents, wholesalers, retailers. They may have comments that are helpful in finally modifying the brand, particularly in its packaging and its selling methods. But the real values here are in getting the involvement of a few key people, and in revealing what problems and prejudices have to be overcome to ensure that the new brand moves smoothly into distribution. The danger of doing this, of course, is that news of the new brand will get back to competitors a

160

less dramatic way this is happening in many markets. It would be difficult, for instance, to sell a really cheap range of cosmetics; most drivers buy a higher grade of petrol than their cars need (and this does not stop them wanting trading stamps with it); the clothes market, because clothes have social as well as personal values, constantly shows both mechanisms working—from Marks & Spencer to Dior.

It seems fairly clear that price indicates both cost and quality to industrial buyers too, although the balance may be a little different. Industrial buying decisions, on all the evidence, are just as quirky and emotional as those of consumers, even though the myth of the rational and omniscient industrial buyer dies hard.

Another of the contributions of Gabor and his colleagues to new product pricing has been his demonstration[1] that, despite the well-known problems about relying on what people say they would pay regularly for anything that is new to them, there are certain conditions in which the answers to hypothetical shopping situations correspond very closely to real life.

Against this background, how does the project manager work out the best price for his new brand? It will depend partly on how functionally new the brand is. Clearly, if it is operating in a well-defined market, it will be much more constrained than if it is competing with substitutes whose nature is very different. This means that the functionally new brand has a wider range of options, but the final decision is rather less critical.

For the pioneering brand, there are two basic approaches, which Joel Dean[2] called the skimming price and the penetration price. The skimming price is one which is relatively high, and skims off the cream of the market. Dean, in fact, suggests that a very rough rule of thumb in the US has been a retail price three or four times the unit production cost. (This falls into the cost-plus trap, but there is more excuse for the pioneering brand, which has few market-place points of reference.) The penetration price is one which is intended to be low enough to lead to immediate acceptance of the new brand by a high proportion of the potential buyers.

It is fairly clear that, in general, the skimming price is a better starting point for a pioneering new brand. It is very much easier to reduce prices later than to put them up. If the brand is a real pioneer, early demand is likely to be fairly restricted and may not be very price-sensitive; this has particularly been the case with consumer durables

[1] GABOR, A., GRANGER, C. W. J., and SOWTER, A. P., "Real and hypothetical shop situations in market research", *Journal of Marketing Research*, August 1970.
[2] DEAN, J., *Managerial Economics* (New Jersey, Prentice-Hall Inc., 1951); "Pricing policies for new products", *Harvard Business Review*, November–December 1960; "Pricing pioneering products", *Journal of Industrial Economics*, July 1969.

like refrigerators, automatic washing machines, dishwashers, colour television and so on. A brand of perceived high quality is better based for launching a later segmented range than a mass-market brand. And of course a skimming price, with an appropriate sales target, represents a lower risk and a lower investment than a penetration price. The danger, as always with lower-risk ventures, is that a competitor may come in and scoop the market with a penetration price.

Just where the range of skimming to penetration prices lies for the pioneering new brand can really only be set by judgement, and modified by market-place experiment. It will change over time, in any case. People simply do not know how much they would be prepared to pay for a genuine novelty, and while it is always worth asking them, results of price questions have to be treated very cautiously. Usually they undervalue novelties very considerably. The only guidelines really are the estimated unit cost and the price of the nearest substitute, but both are fairly rough. What, for instance, was the substitute for frozen fish? Fresh fish or canned fish or meat or baked beans or what? Frozen fish could not be priced too far away from any of these, but of course they represent a fairly wide range themselves. The frozen food business is a good example of the real-life problems of pricing for a pioneer product. A truly skimming price would simply not have got enough frozen food cabinets into the retail trade to establish a market, while a truly penetration price would never have recovered the huge investments in plant, cold storage and refrigerated vehicles.

Where the new brand is moving into an established market and there is a fairly general awareness of prices, the range between skimming and penetration is smaller. Everything depends on the skill with which added values have been built into the new brand. The same principles apply, but research can be much more valuable in pinpointing the right price, by establishing the current range.

Camay toilet soap showed the possibilities in an established market. Camay was Procter & Gamble's first entrant into the UK toilet-soap market, which was then dominated by Unilever and Colgate with their mass-market brands (Lux, Lifebuoy, Knights Castile, Palmolive), whose prices were identical—the standard penetration price. Also in the market were brands (Bronnley, Chanel, etc.) with very high skimming prices—they were as much cosmetics or gifts as toilet soaps. Camay entered the market with a "modified skimming" price, 4d per bath size more than the mass-market brands. Backed by heavy and whole-hearted advertising and promotions Camay reached market leadership within its first year. Its higher price indicated quality, and reinforced its more dramatic product qualities (Camay was both more liked and more disliked than other brands) and its excellent advertising ("perfume worth nine guineas an ounce"). After about eighteen months the higher price began to tell, and it was cut to prevailing levels. The reputation for quality and glamour remained, and Camay has been among the market leaders ever since. Several years later Procter & Gamble introduced Fairy toilet soap at a penetration price, 3d per bath size below the standard price. Fairy also briefly became market leader and has remained a major brand.

FIGURE 22. Success for a modified skimming price

Gabor's method for establishing the range of prices acceptable in a market is based on earlier work by Professor Stoetzel,[1] whose view was that anyone intending to buy approaches the market with two limits in mind. The upper limit is the maximum he is prepared to pay for any brand, however good it may be; the lower is the point below which he would have serious doubts about the quality. These limits can be established by simple direct questions which consumers can and do easily answer, such as (to quote Gabor and Granger's[2] example):

1. "If you wanted to buy a tin of soup sufficient for two helpings, which is the highest price you would be prepared to pay?"

2. "Which is the lowest price at which you would still buy—I mean the price below which you would not trust the quality?"

[1] STOETZEL, J., "Le prix comme limite", in *La psychologie économique*, ed. P. L. Reynaud (Paris, 1954).

[2] GABOR, A., and GRANGER, C. W. J., "The pricing of new products", *Scientific Business*, August 1965, p. 6.

The results can, by simple subtraction, be expressed as the percentage of potential customers for a brand at each price named—that is, the number of people for whom each price falls within the acceptable

Market price profile

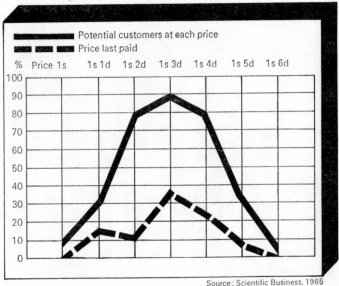

Source: Scientific Business, 1965

FIGURE 23. **Plotting potential customers at each price against what was paid last time can show pricing opportunities (Gabor and Granger)**

range. And the distribution of potential customers can be plotted against the distribution of prices paid for the last brand bought.

This method of establishing the range of prices can be complemented by Gabor and Granger's "indirect" method, which involves asking consumers questions like:

1. "If you went out to get some nylon stockings for yourself, and saw the shade and quality you were looking for, would you take them if the price were x pence?" (If the answer is "yes", go on to next price. If "no", ask:)

2. "Why not? Would you think them too expensive—or too cheap to trust? I will now name a few other prices, could you please just answer either: 'yes, buy' or 'no, too expensive' or 'no, too cheap'."

Experience showed that individuals are able to cope with up to eight or nine different prices; and both the "direct" and the "indirect" methods appear to be internally consistent and a valid indication of people's real attitudes.

These are of course methods for mapping price attitudes and behaviour in the market as a whole. They should certainly be used in the research at the planning stage into consumers and consumption. It is not so clear whether they could be of direct value to pinpointing the optimal price of the new brand, since the most real-life pre-test exposure of the new brand is still very artificial. The buy-response (indirect) method is really more suitable for "backward-cost-pricing" than for finding the right price after the brand has been developed. But it certainly seems worth trying the "indirect" method at the second stage of the pre-test. That is, asking "If you found Z (the new brand) in the shops and the price was x pence, would you buy it?", and so on. The results would be compared with the general market findings. Almost certainly the stimulus of being interviewed, curiosity, desire to try something new once would mean an exaggerated willingness to pay high prices. But this could be taken into account— increasingly accurately with experience—and there would be both a wider range of prices considered and a firmer basis for comparison than is usually the case in pre-test research into willingness to buy at stated prices.

In any case, as Gabor makes clear, these measures aim to be a reliable tool to help new-brand pricing decisions, not a mechanical process. More than most consumer research, the design and interpretation of pricing research require expert knowledge. The actual fixing of the price will remain a matter of imagination and judgement.

PRODUCTION PLANNING AND COSTING

Throughout the whole of the evaluation stage a production plan is being worked out. As we have seen, the whole stage needs to be planned in outline before the critical path network can be set up, and of course the production planning depends on the scale of marketing envisaged. Fundamentally the production planning for new brands is no different from planning for going brands; it is just that there are rather more uncertainties, and so every step has to be thought out carefully, rather than past actions being followed almost by instinct.

This is the time when machinery is installed, tested and tuned; people are trained to use it; quality-control standards and machine rates are established; the final specifications of the product are established and written into the rule book; a technical service for the new brand is set up, if necessary; raw-material contracts are placed; and there is a continuous process of refining the cost accounting.

167

This is all fairly routine work for the production department, but a lot of errors can creep in at this stage. The interdependence of product design, packaging, sales volume, costing and production mean that the production member of the project team and the project manager have between them a very important task in making the most of the existing facilities and working methods of the production department, while maintaining both the integrity and the impetus of the new brand.

MARKET PLANNING AND SALES/PROFITS FORECASTS

There is a parallel operation in the marketing department, where a marketing plan is being drawn up, with sales and profit forecasts, budgets, sales campaigns and so on. In many ways, it will be a perfectly conventional marketing plan of the sort that the marketing department turns out every year. In some ways, it will be easier to work out, since the essential elements of the product mix (product, pack design, advertising and style of communication) have already been developed and tested. What remains to be planned is essentially the distribution mix—the selling methods, sales force, sales training, incentives, aids, trade meetings, introductory discounts; the price structure; a data-processing system for sales figures and market research; transport and distribution methods, case sizes, minimum orders and drops; special methods of distribution, such as sampling or coupons; trade and/or consumer promotions. The planning and execution of these can make all the difference between success and failure; but the methods and principles are the same as for marketing established brands.

There are some areas which need special attention, not normally given to going brands. First, there is a special need to double-check those legal requirements, Government regulations and industry codes which cover the presentation, description and promotion of the new brand. Secondly, the market research set up to monitor progress has to be particularly carefully planned, and will almost certainly be more expensive than the company's norm for going brands. Thirdly, experiments—particularly pricing and promotion experiments—need to be more carefully built into the plan than for a going brand.

Fourthly, and most important, the real problem in drawing up this marketing plan is the basic uncertainty about the likely scale of the operation, the amount of promotion needed and the internal breakdown of the marketing budget. There is no series of previous figures to act as a base for forecasts. Even here the techniques of marketing planning are the usual ones and the broad outlines of the operation have been envisaged ever since the basic choice of market; it is the shortage of precise numbers that makes it difficult. If the new brand can be thought of as fitting into an established market, it is a matter of making judgements—based on the hints about the competitive position of the new brand from the pre-test and other research—about the likely market share; its likely effect on market growth; the share of advertising needed to sustain that share plus the "investment" amount needed to reach it; the degree of discounting necessary, based on pre-testing on retailers, to ensure distribution. Where the brand is an entirely new concept, then the nearest substitute can act as a very rough guide, and forecasts have to be based on pre-test indications of likely penetration and likely buying frequency.

These calculations of scale are inevitably judgmental, and this has been one of the main reasons why manufacturers of new brands use test markets. The marketing plan has been one scaled down to a limited region, partly to reduce the size of the problem if errors of forecasting have been made and partly to ensure more accurate forecasts for national marketing. What is not quite so clear is just how much test marketing really helps either of these objectives.

TEST MARKETING OR PILOT MARKETING?

The question of whether to test-market a new brand or to launch it nationally has never been easy, and it is not getting any easier, despite a vast body of literature on the subject. On the whole, the simpler textbooks advocate it as the correct course for marketing men, and on the whole the more sophisticated theorists and practical men have doubts and reservations. Two brief quotations give the flavour of the discussion. On the one hand: "The only way a manufacturer or distributor can really know whether consumers will buy the product is to offer it for sale. . . . A programme of test marketing must be carried out with a methodology, and on a scale, which will permit reasonably accurate projection of its results".[1] On the other hand: "Test marketing is warranted if, and only if, it will probably save money for the company . . . (It) is not only expensive, but it also has its limitations, not the least of which is the competitive disadvantage of telling your competitors all about your plans. Therefore, test marketing should be visualized as a last resort of sorts. . . ."[2]

There is a second question to be asked, in some ways more important. If the new brand is to be launched in a limited area, what is

[1] LADIK, F., KENT, L., NAHL, P. C., "Test marketing of new consumer products", *Journal of Marketing*, April 1966, p. 29.
[2] O'HANLON, J. J., "Experimental marketing: A US businessman puts it on test", *Marketing*, October 1970, p. 36.

the real purpose of this? There are two basic possibilities here, and it is very important in planning to distinguish them.[1]

First, there is what E. J. Davis (in *Experimental Marketing*[2]— much the most sensible and comprehensive book available on test marketing) has called the *projectable test launch*. This is the true test market, a small-scale operation designed to provide an exact simulation of the large-scale. The object is to be able to predict the scale of national sales reasonably accurately. At the extreme, this is in order to make go/no-go decisions about the new brand. More often, it is to help detailed planning of production, distribution, sales and budgeting for national marketing.

Secondly, there is the *pilot launch*. Here, as with the operation of a pilot plant, the objective is essentially experimentation. This will be the first time that all the elements of the marketing mix are brought together in real-life conditions, and it is the first time that the factory will be producing continuously. Apart from the possibility that individual elements will behave rather differently in real life from the pre-test, the interactions between them (for instance, between price and perceived product quality after repeated purchase) can never be predicted very accurately in a pre-test. The final modifications to the mix, which may make a big difference to the success of the new brand, need real-life conditions before they can be made with any confidence. A pilot marketing operation allows this to be done on a small scale, so that the national launching is done with a perfected brand.

The basic danger of test marketing is that it loses time and alerts competitors. Time is lost particularly when the test is being used as a projectable test launch for a go/no-go decision; if the company is going to wait until the results are really clear before ordering the machinery for a national introduction, then there are very few businesses in which that does not mean at least a year's delay. The desire for secrecy and lead time over competitors no doubt is often overdone; the company is trying to build a lasting new business, not get a quick temporary advantage. All the same, the delays of test marketing have often spoilt what might have been successful businesses. There is a subtler danger too: test marketing can be used subconsciously as another way of putting off the really difficult decisions, and the whole project can lose impetus.

The question that the project manager has to ask is whether the values of the test market in reducing investment risks or improving the new brand outweigh the risks of delay and loss of surprise.

---

[1] ACHENBAUM, A. A., "The purpose of market testing", American Marketing Association, 47th National Conference, June 1964.
[2] DAVIS, E. J., *Experimental marketing* (London, Nelson 1970).

Projecting from Test Markets

The idea that a region can be selected so as to be typical of the whole nation and that sales can be accurately projected from one to the other was jolted badly by some simple analysis in a classic paper by Jack Gold in 1964.[1] He took the results from retail audits on seven established brands in six regions which were popular test regions, and used three different methods for projecting the sales results to national level. He found that the range of error for projections went from an underestimate of 49 per cent to an overestimate of 80 per cent. To put it a little more operationally, when one test market was used, in about half the cases the projections were more than 25 per cent out. Each of the three methods used gave both underestimates and overestimates, and so did five of the six regions. What most improved the projections was the use of more than one test region. For instance, only 35 per cent of the projections fell within 15 per cent of the true national figure, when one test market was used; but when three were used, 60 per cent were within 15 per cent.

Any company with reasonable retail audit data can try the same exercise; at the simplest level, by asking how good is market share in each region at predicting the national market share. For most companies the answer is: not very. Gold's analysis, in dealing with known results and an undisturbed market, was a much less severe test for projections than a real test market. He showed that brand share is a better basis for projection than sales per head of the population or income levels or relationship with sales of known brands. But for brand share projections to work, there has to be a fairly accurate figure for total national sales, and it is unusual to have this when entering a new market. It will be relatively rare too for the entry of a new brand to make no difference to the size of the market or the activity in it.

This last point really raises something rather more fundamental. The statistical problems of projectability can be lessened by using several test regions (though of course this can somewhat defeat the object of the exercise—to test on a small scale). And Davis's method of projecting by "standardizing" brand shares[2] seems to lead to more accurate results. What raises a new problem is the undoubted fact that the accuracy of projection will depend on the degree of experimental discipline in the test market. In very simple terms, it will depend on the extent to which conditions are "normal" in the test region. And it will depend on there being no changes made to the new brand or the marketing mix between test and national marketing.

[1] GOLD, J. A., "Testing test market predictions", *Journal of Marketing Research*, August 1964.
[2] DAVIS, E. J., *Experimental marketing*, p. 144 (London, Nelson 1970).

171

In fact, these requirements are both unrealistic and unhelpful.

First, it is very unlikely that conditions will be "normal" in the test region. The very fact that it is a test and that the careers of the project team and prospects for the company will be affected by its results make it unreasonable to expect a cool scientific detachment. Even though it is possible to guard the extremes (like the case quoted by Davis of eighteen marketing and sales people operating in a test area normally run by four), it is hardly possible or even desirable to limit deep involvement in the test. Competitive activity is unlikely to be normal, either. It is very common and indeed sensible for manufacturers to spoil each other's test markets by mounting short-term promotions or deep price cuts at an intensity that could not conceivably be afforded nationally or over a long period. If one is faced with a potentially dangerous new competitor, what better than to try to strangle it at birth?

There are also technical problems involved in scaling down a proposed national operation. Press and colour magazine advertising cannot easily be scaled down, and there is the problem of working out on what basis to scale down advertising expenditure—number of impacts, cost per head of population and share of national expenditure all tend to give different answers. There are problems with the precise coverage and the policies of wholesalers and multiple retailers. There are problems even with the special help given by the test market packages offered by certain television contractors, which are not reproduced nationally. All in all, it is hard not to agree with Davis that "test marketing tends to be statistically invalid from the start".

Secondly, it is very questionable whether it is worth sticking rigidly to the brand and marketing mix of the test area simply in order to be able to project the national sales level more accurately. If the test reveals problems of production, distribution, promotion, product stability or any of the other things that can go wrong, it would be ridiculous not to try to put them right for national marketing. Yet it will be impossible to say what effect the improvement will have on sales. The inevitable conclusion is that the more effective the pilot element, the less effective the projection element.

Pilot Marketing

On the other hand, small-scale marketing as a pilot can be very valuable. First, in a mechanical way; secondly, acting for marketing in the way that pilot plant does for production.

The mechanical values are all too often forgotten, but they are often the more important. The pilot marketing stage is the first opportunity to go through the whole process of buying, receiving and storing bulk raw materials; working through the production learning curve; continuous high-speed packaging; warehousing, transporting and delivery in bulk of the finished product. It is rare for there to be no bugs in the system at all, and very often they can lead to damaging delays or ill-will from suppliers or customers. It is clearly a good thing to get them out of the system before large-scale marketing.

The analogy of pilot plant production makes the marketing values clear. Production engineers do not run pilots simply to be able to predict output; the object is, by taking intermediate measures, to refine and improve the system. In the same way the pilot marketing stage can be used to examine individual elements in the system. What are the distribution and display levels; are they of the scale and type envisaged; and what sort of approach or special incentive seems best for improving them? How have the salesmen performed; has their basic sales story been understood and accepted; if not, where has it gone wrong? Have the people taking up the new brand been the target group envisaged? Have they understood the advertising in the right way? Has the advertising registered with enough of them? Has there been high enough initial sampling; does a coupon or a free sample or an introductory offer work best? Has there been a high enough repeat-purchasing rate? If not, what are the attitudes to the brand of once-only triers; is it a matter of apathy or is there something wrong with the brand? How do attitudes relate to those shown in pre-test?

In other words, there are two sorts of marketing question to be asked at the pilot stage. The first aims to monitor all the links in the distribution chain, from warehouse to final consumer, in order to improve weaknesses. The second employs some of the questions used in the pre-test to confirm that the new brand itself is performing as it promised to do.

If this pilot approach is going to include specific experiments—say, two different recommended retail prices—then normally it will require two separate marketing areas, or at least one (like the Southern ITV area) which can be easily split. Clearly costs and scale of operations will prevent very elaborate experiments. But there is a lot that can be done with test towns, provided that the objectives are clear, the experiments bold, the measurements appropriate and the approach open-minded and ingenious. This is particularly true where the experiment is dealing with a sub-system; for instance, comparing two different retailer incentives, as measured by initial distribution, or coupon against no coupon, as measured by penetration after four weeks. This sort of experiment, since it is completed in a short period, allows follow-up work and successive modifications, without fear of invalidating results.

Another proviso about this sort of pilot marketing is fairly obvious;

there must be plenty of research, and sales must be capable of detailed analysis. In order to answer, for instance, the questions listed on page 173, the project team would require retail audit data (distribution, display, shop purchases and sales); detailed distribution and delivery returns from the sales side; research into retailers' attitudes; consumer panel data (penetration, prices paid and repeat purchase); consumer research—both qualitative (understanding of advertising, attitudes of once-only buyers) and quantitative (advertising impact, attitudes to brand related to competitors). This sounds a lot, and it would not be cheap. But it would obviously be ridiculous to mount a pilot marketing operation, and then not be able to learn anything more from it than the overall level of sales.

Mini-tests

The values of small-scale marketing as a pilot rather than as a project-able test launch help to put mini-tests into perspective. Mini-tests are small-scale operations which are closer to real life than the pre-test, but do not involve real marketing and so have two great advantages over it. First, they are much cheaper; and secondly, they do not— with any luck—alert the competition.

The principle of mini-tests is to set up a panel of captive consumers, to simulate advertising and promotion to them, and then give them the opportunity to buy brands in the relevant market at normal prices over a period of time. Direct mail and salesmen calling have been used for this; or a regular catalogue plus telephone ordering system from a warehouse. The best method is probably the mobile shop, such as the system operated in the UK by Research Bureau Limited,[1] which has two consumer panels of five hundred housewives each. They are visited once a week by the mobile shop, which offers all the brands in the product field. Display and advertising are simulated by a four-weekly brochure. The basic measures taken are of penetration and repeat-purchase, and these can of course be compared with normal consumer panel data for the market. The splitting of the panel enables experiments to be done with validity, and the great advantage over the pre-test is that the influences of price and repeat-buying are investigated.

While there are clearly values here—in particular, mini-tests are a cheap and inconspicuous way of getting rid of gross error—there are considerable limitations. If it is hard to project national sales from a test market, it must be even harder to project from a mini-test, which is still a long way from real life. At the same time, it is not of great value for pilot marketing, since it makes no attempt to simulate the

[1] PYMONT, B., "The RBL mini-test market", Market Research Society conference, 1969.

real-life distribution system. In fact, the mini-test should really be thought of as a supplement to the pre-test, rather than an alternative to small-scale marketing.

Deciding about Test Marketing

The right decision for any new brand will clearly depend on circumstances, the market concerned and the type of production machinery involved. In many ways, the production side has the most influence on choice. There is normally no question of test marketing a car, because the production line is so expensive and takes so long to lay down that the test cars would be prohibitively costly and the later national cars would be out of date. Equally, in some chocolate confectionery lines, investment in the mould cycle is much the same for a national operation as for a test, and this is one argument for national introduction. At the other end of the scale, cigarette machinery is much the same for a whole range of possible new brands, but the impossibility of simulating national press media and national excitement in an area argues against test marketing.

But it is possible, all the same, to come to some general conclusions. It seems clear that truly accurate projection from a test market is going to be rare, but there are a great many new brands for which a projection that is within 50 per cent would be better than nothing. At the same time, the values of pilot marketing are very clear and it would be a very confident project team that felt it had nothing more to learn after the pre-test. The most sensible course, in most circumstances, seems to be:

(a) Plan and use small-scale marketing specifically as a pilot, with built-in experiments.

(b) Get from it a quick broad measure of success or failure, remembering that the proper question is: "Are we likely to be able to build a worth-while business from this?"

(c) Use early indicative results, with pinches of salt, to help plan national investment and production schedules.

(d) Depending on the perceived importance of lead time over competitors, spread to further regions (or even nationally in one go).

REVIEW

There is a final review before the new brand is actually put into its pilot market. On the face of it, this is management's last chance to modify or stop the new brand before a great deal of money is invested in advertising and marketing. In fact, it is not quite as simple as that,

175

since the decision to invest in at least some machinery must already have been taken; there will already be fairly heavy cost penalites in quitting now. It is clear that decision-making has been a fairly continuous matter ever since the choice of markets and setting of market priorities.

As before, the most important part of this review is the examination by management of all the work done at the evaluation stage, in particular the production plan, the costing, the pilot marketing plan, and the forecasts of sales and profits deriving from them. This will mean a lot of work for top management. It is no use their simply reading the summaries or the last line, and saying yes or no. It is a matter of getting immersed in all stages of the work done and the arguments put forward. Has the evaluation been thorough and soundly based? Are the arguments realistic and logical? Has there been too much caution, or is there too much wishful thinking? Is the project team's assessment of the risks valid? Is top management prepared to take these risks? Does there really look to be a worth-while business here, and when?

It is reasonable that management at this stage should ask for some clear figures on which to make their decisions. The new product literature mostly suggests a choice between the alternatives of new brand A, new brand B or no new brand. And that the basis of the choice should be the long-run return on investment, adjusted by discounted cash flow principles. It seems a reasonable request. But even at this stage it does not really work that way.

Estimates of sales, costs and prices are still very speculative, and quite minor variations, particularly in price, will dramatically affect the return on investment. While it is good for people to quantify their estimates, a guess is still a guess, even when surrounded by decision theory and Bayesian statistics. These techniques can be very valuable, provided that everyone involved understands them; otherwise they can be extremely dangerous, by tempting managements to make decisions not on the basis of examining the whole new-brand development work done so far, but of deciding which of two numbers is the larger.

There is another reason why a choice between alternatives at this stage is unrealistic. As has been clear throughout, commitment is vital to a new brand's success. This means that it cannot normally be sensible to ask a project team to hedge its bets by producing a number of alternative new brands for weeding out at this stage. It is quite possible to have variations on a theme, but it is asking too much of people to expect a deep commitment to each of several alternatives. Equally, it cannot make too much sense to have separate project teams working on separate new brands, with the idea that there will be a grand competition before test marketing and that there will be only one winner.

176

The decision-making process emerges as a continuous one, with the three screening reviews put into the flow diagram more as a discipline than to suggest that they are the only occasions for management decision. In fact, the most important element in the final go/no-go decision on the new brand was taken as a result of the economic analysis in the choice of markets. It was decided then that it looked as if the company could build a profitable business in market A; and continually since then the questions have been asked: "On the basis of what we now know, does it still look as if we can build a good business in market A? Do we still think we can achieve in the long run the profit levels that are current in market A or better? Are we still prepared to make the marketing investment needed to reach those levels?" Return on investment, in other words, is used more as a way of thinking than as a precise calculation; and market A can be abandoned at any stage, as new information comes in.

But there can be no certainty. DuPont's views on likely profits clearly encouraged them to embark on Corfam. It turned out in the end to be a very expensive failure; but right up to the point of withdrawal there could have been changes in the situation that radically altered the return on investment. DuPont are still likely to make a good business out of synthetic leather, or something very like it, one day. Equally, the original profit projections for Mr. Kipling were fairly dramatically optimistic—indeed, realistic ones might even have jeopardized the whole venture. But the Mr. Kipling business four years later looks very different; it has been modified over time, is now far more efficient and is returning a good profit. The critical point is that it is no flash-in-the-pan new brand; it is a solid new business of great long-term potential.

So the new brand finally goes into pilot marketing. It has been developed mainly by intuition and creativity; and even now it is backed by judgement in the face of uncertainties. But it would be quite unrealistic to expect anything else. The way to improve the success rate is not to look for some miracle methods of eliminating bad risks or of choosing between alternatives; but to work out a coherent theory and apply it throughout the whole development programme.

Annotated Reading List

Not many people will have the time to follow up the hundred-odd references in the text. So here is a short-list of just twenty titles. Like all such selections, it is a very personal choice. These are the books and articles that I have found particularly comprehensive or illuminating or stimulating:

1. ACHILLADELIS, B., JERVIS, P., and ROBERTSON, A., *A study of success and failure in industrial innovation: Report on project SAPPHO to SRC* (Science Research Council, August 1971).
   A fascinating report on twenty-nine paired comparisons of successful and unsuccessful attempts to innovate in two industries—chemicals and scientific instruments. Includes an excellent bibliography on innovation and a summary of the results of thirty previous case studies.

2. ANSOFF, H. I., and STEWART, J. M., "Strategies for a technology-based business", *Harvard Business Review*, November–December 1967.
   Detailed analysis of the effects on companies of accelerating technological change, discussion of the strategic options open to them and the implications for management.

3. BARNETT. N. L., "Beyond market segmentation", *Harvard Business Review*, January–February 1969.
   Review of the various market segmentation techniques used for developing new consumer products. Notes that none of them seems satisfactory, and suggests that we may need a different approach.

4. BURNS, T., and STALKER, G. M., *The management of innovation* (London, Tavistock Publications, 1961).
   Arising from a study of twenty companies, mainly in electronics, this book deals with the demands that technical innovation makes on managements, and the sort of organization that seems best for it.

5. DAVIS, E. J., *Experimental marketing* (London, Nelson, 1970).
   Comprehensive and wholly practical guide to test-marketing and other forms of market experiment. Simply, the best book on the subject.

6. DAVIS, E. J., *The sales curves of new products* (Market Research Society conference, 1964, and J. Walter Thompson Company Limited, 1965).
   Study of forty-four new brands in grocery and chemist shops. One of the few attempts to look at new brands in reasonable numbers, it shows that their sales patterns have important similarities.

7. DE BONO, E., *The use of lateral thinking* (London, Jonathan Cape, 1967).
   Stimulating analysis of the vertical and lateral modes of thinking, with many suggestions for developing innovative approaches to problems. And the methods really work.

8. GABOR, A., and GRANGER, C. W. J., "The pricing of new products", *Scientific Business*, August 1965.
   A sensible theoretical approach to how consumers respond to prices, with research methods to match. The only really practical work that has been done on pricing new brands.

9. GARDNER, B. B., and LEVY, S. J., "The product and the brand", *Harvard Business Review*, March–April 1955.
   Classic article on the difference between products and brands, and the need for qualitative research into consumers' motives.

10. GORDON, W. J. J., "Operational approach to creativity", *Harvard Business Review*, November–December 1956.
    Individualistic account of how intuitive processes can be stimulated on a larger scale by managements.

11. GREENHALGH, C., Generating new product ideas, ESOMAR congress, 1971, and *Admap*, September, October and November 1971.
    Comprehensive review of the techniques used for generating new product ideas and the literature on the subject.

12. KUEHN, A. A., and DAY, R. L., "Strategy of product quality", *Harvard Business Review*, November–December 1962.
    Suggests more subtle analyses of product tests than manufacturers usually do and raises many important questions on the importance and meaning of "product quality".

13. LEVITT, T., "Marketing myopia", *Harvard Business Review*, July–August 1960.
    Basic text on the need to look at markets from the consumer's point of view, not just the producer's.

179

14. LEVITT, T., *The marketing mode* (New York, McGraw-Hill Book Company, 1969).
   Not a how-to-do-it book on marketing, but much the most stimulating and provocative treatment of the whole subject.

15. MEDAWAR, P. B., *Induction and intuition in scientific thought* (London, Methuen, 1969).
   A simple but fundamental analysis of the true nature of the scientific method.

16. PARFITT, J. H., and COLLINS, B. J. K., "The use of consumer panels for brand-share prediction", *Journal of Marketing Research*, May 1968.
   Analysis from consumer panel data of the effect on a brand's sales of the number of people buying and the repeat-buying rate; the patterns set out here are very important both for early prediction and for understanding the nature of new brands.

17. QUINN, J. B., "Technological forecasting", *Harvard Business Review*, March–April 1967.
   Very clear review of the purposes, methods and values of technological forecasting, and its implications for organization and data collection.

18. SAMPSON, P., "Can consumers create new products?", *Journal of the Market Research Society*, January 1970.
   How research can be organized to tap ordinary consumers' creative abilities in looking for new product ideas.

19. SCHON, D. A., The Reith lectures, *The Listener*, 19 November–24 December 1970.
   Wide-ranging discussion of innovation, its relationship to changes in today's society, and the problems it poses for the conventionally structured organization.

20. STEWART, J. B., "Functional features in product strategy", *Harvard Business Review*, March–April 1959.
   Exhaustive study from the US of the importance and exploitation of new functional features in brands.

Index

Page references followed by n *indicate footnotes*

ACHILLADELIS, B., 41n, 178
Added values, 9–16
Adhesives, 114–7, 128–9
Ad hoc consumer surveys, 85
Advertising, 136–7
  testing, 140
Advertising Planning Index, 21
Aerosols, 75–6
After Eight mints, 13, 74
Air travel, 73
Andrex toilet paper, 10–14
Ansoff, H. I., 67, 68, 178
Applications engineering, 68
Assets, *see* Company assets
Attitude research, 88–91, 113
Attwood Consumer Panel, 19, 21, 111, 112
Augmented-product concept, 14
Automatic Interaction Detector programme, 94
Automobile industry, 141

BABYCHAM, 13, 68
Barnett, N. L., 92n, 93n, 178
Batchelors Foods, 37, 83
Behaviour of new brands, 16–22
Berg, Thomas L., 35
Bird's Eye Foods, 13, 73–4
Blind product tests, 89, 137
Bono, Edward de, 105, 179
Booz, Allen and Hamilton, 40–1
Bowater-Scott Company, 10, 11
Bradford University, Management Centre, 81
Brainstorming, 105
Brand manager, 29
Brand names, 134–6
Brand personality, 14, 91

Brands *v.* products, 7–8
British Bakeries, 110–14, 125, 135
British Market Research Bureau (BMRB), 17, 112
Burns, T., 69n, 178
Buying decisions, 85–7

CADBURY LTD., 73, 81–2
Cakes, 110–14, 125
  see also Mr. Kipling cakes
Camay toilet soap, 164–5
Canned peas, 83
Car industry, 141
Check-lists of idea-stimulating devices, 106
Clothes cleaning, 103
Clucas technique, 140
Collins, B. J. K., 19n, 156n, 180
Communications for new brands, 130–1, 140–1, 153
Company assets, 60–6
  British Bakeries, 111
  Dunlop Adhesives, 114–15
Competitors' activities, monitoring, 100
Consumer group discussions, 101–2
Consumer panel data, 19–21, 85, 111, 112
Consumer research, 129, 155
  British Bakeries, 112–13
  Dunlop Adhesives, 115
Consumers—
  appeal of new brands to, 23–7
  behaviour and attitudes of, 84–97
  ideas from, 101–2
  relations with, 62, 63, 64
Contact adhesives, 128–9

181